A
Feast of Flowers

Francesca Tillona and
Cynthia Strowbridge

Funk & Wagnalls
New York

Dedicated to the memory of our mothers

Contents

Introduction

§ The modern American woman uses flowers primarily for their loveliness and fragrance—to decorate her living room, to thank her hostess of the night before, to mark a sentimental occasion, to cheer up a friend who is under the weather. But usually the closest she comes to bringing together flowers and food is in the placing of a centerpiece on the dinner table.

In other times and other places, however, flowers were treasured for more than their beauty and perfume. They were believed to be endowed with many kinds of medicinal, cosmetic, and—above all—nutritional properties.

The ancient Romans, for example, believed they could ward off drunkenness by floating fresh rose petals in their wine cups; and in view of the frequency with which those cups were allegedly refilled, they were well advised to seek such preventive measures. Even earlier, the Greeks found violets valuable as a soporific, a remedy for dizziness, and a cure for persistent headaches.

In the Middle Ages, the Maybowle, flavored with woodruff, was believed to be a potent purifier of the blood. The sweet-scented leaves of the woodruff plant were added to other beverages too, rendering them, according to herbalists, "cordial, stomachic, tonic, diuretic, and pectoral."

Because flowers were believed to have so many valuable qualities, it is understandable that some effort would have been made to preserve them through the seasons in which fresh blossoms were not readily available. It is not surprising, therefore, that ways were found to dry flowers, to pickle or candy them, and to extract their essence in waters and oils. A reference to distilled rose water occurs as early as the second century B.C., in the writings of the Greek poet Nicander. In the Middle East, flower waters had already found their way into conserves and preserves by the eighth century A.D. And throughout Europe, flowers and flower products became indispensable not only in the preparation of food but also in the concoction of cosmetic and medicinal potions of all kinds.

The most complete records of the use of flowers are to be found in the cookbooks and collections of "household hints" which began to be published in England in the late sixteenth and seventeenth centuries.

From Francis Bacon we learn that the leaf of the borage "hath an excellent *f*pirit to repre*f*s the fuliginous vapours of du*f*ky Melancholy and *f*o cure Madne*f*s . . . ," while for John Swan it "increa*f*eth Wit, & Memorie, [&] engendereth good blood. . . ."

Mixtures with bases of flower oils and waters were used to clear bloodshot eyes, relieve pain, stop bleeding, dissolve stones, regulate the digestion, and mitigate the effects of passionate anger or passionate love. The ladies used similar mixtures to bleach freckles, clear complexions, color hair, and smooth out wrinkles. Thus in England, as throughout the Continent, flowers held an important place both in the medicine chest and in the toilette.

But far more important, for our purposes, was the place they held in the kitchen. Flower conserves had been introduced in England through trade with the East during and between the Crusades—and perhaps even earlier. By the sixteenth century, flowers had found their way into all kinds of English foods and beverages.

Lavender was used to color and flavor confectioneries, wines, and sugars. Violets—fresh, dried, or distilled—were added to wines, conserves, and liqueurs. Marigolds, less expensive and more easily available than saffron, were popular for stews, broths, and custards. Daylilies, the mysterious flowers that usually bloom for a single day, were not only added to soups and stews but were also prepared by themselves as side dishes. In England as on the Continent, sunflowers were a staple. The seeds were prized as seasoning for cakes, cookies, and pastries; the buds were pickled and used as a relish; the blossoms were added to salads or cooked and dressed as a side dish. The leaves of the lemon geranium were used—sparingly—as flavoring for jellies, custards, and rice puddings. And, of course, the ever-popular rose—in all its multiple varieties —was used to color, flavor, and perfume everything from poultry to pies and sherbets to soups.

From the English household books of the sixteenth, seventeenth, and eighteenth centuries, and from their French and Italian counterparts, came the idea for this volume. We were intrigued at first when, quite by accident, we came across Gervase Markham's 1615 recipe for mutton with "violet leaves, succory, ſtrawberry leaves, [and] Mary-gold flowers." Violet leaves? Strawberry leaves? Marigold flowers???

But we soon found other recipes and other authors to confirm the use of these—to us—outlandish ingredients. We experimented, gingerly at first and out of sheer curiosity. Like John Evelyn, who recorded some of his failures in *Acetaria*, we were not always successful. One problem was the disconcerting casualness of these antique recipes. "Take a pretty quantity of sugar," suggests one writer; "add a good handfull of orange-flowers," recommends another, "and beat for a good while," says a third. We watched custards curdle, cakes collapse, and soufflés sink while we struggled to adjust these rather whimsical directions for quantities and timing to terms intelligible to the modern cook. Still, we became caught in the same kind of fascination that impels some collectors of other things antique —the urge to reach out from this era of computer cards and TV dinners to the more romantic time of parchment scrolls and royal banquets.

As we assembled our final manuscript, we had to keep in mind several considerations. First, not all the flowers called for in antique recipes exist in North America. When an English author calls for "a peck of cowslips," for instance, he means something quite different from the American variety. So our first step was the "Americanization" of the recipes, adapting them to the use of flowers readily available in this country.

We also modernized the terminology of some of the older recipes, to make them more relevant to modern utensils and procedures. When certain ingredients called for in the old recipes had become rare or no longer popular, we substituted modern equivalents. Quantities, timing, and directions have been altered to suit modern cookbook usage and the modern housewife. We have also added suggestions for other ways in which American flowers may be incorporated in contemporary recipes. The medicinal and cosmetic recipes are presented in their original form, since these are not seriously offered for use, yet are a part of the picture. Because these came from many sources and periods there are many inconsistencies in spelling and in use of the old-style "s."

Our book, therefore, is intended not only for the dedicated cook, or the dedicated collector of cookbooks, but also for those who have an interest in things of the past, and for those adventurous souls who will enjoy exploring the "new" element of flowers and flower products. We hope it will bring to your dinner table a new and pleasing spectrum of color, fragrance, and flavor.

Acknowledgments

§ Our thanks to four expert cooks who contributed suggestions that were most useful in the preparation of this book. These counselors and friends are Winifred Strowbridge, Mollie Laniado, Lucy Coniglione, and Mary Leonard.

We appreciate the help of our editor, who encouraged us during the writing of this book. His ideas proved invaluable in shaping the finished version of *A Feast of Flowers*.

A Feast of Flowers

Medicinal and
Cosmetic Recipes

§ The "recipes" in this section are not for the dinner table, but for the "medicine chest" and the
toilette table. They come from the same books that
were our sources for the food recipes.

Most of the antique books from which we took
our recipes are not ordinary cookbooks. They are,
in effect, an offshoot of the "courtesy books" that
flourished on the Continent and in England in the
sixteenth century. Books designed to instruct the
prince in royal responsibilities, the courtier in dip-
lomatic procedures, and the suitor in amorous tradition may have led subtly, but not illogically, to
books designed to instruct the housewife in her
function as mainstay of the home.

As such, they could not be confined to mere collections of food recipes, for the woman in the six-
teenth- and seventeenth-century household was re-

sponsible for much more than simply preparing meals. She was nurse and pharmacist in times of family illness, and her own cosmetician and hair-dresser as well. And these functions were usually jealously guarded, no matter how many servants she might have had at her disposal. Accordingly, these early books, which are really "manuals for house-wives," usually included large sections on the preparation of medicines and cosmetics.

Because we desired so strongly to preserve the flavor of these old books, we decided that our own modernized version of traditional flower cookery would not be complete without at least a sampling of medicinal and cosmetic recipes.

We cannot guarantee that they will be effective in restoring health or preserving beauty. We include them because they represent interesting and, in some cases, surprising uses of flowers and flower products.

Medicinal Uses

For the Swimming or dizzinefs in the Head . . .
Take of Agnus caſtus, or broom-wort, and of Camomile dryed, of each two drams mixed with the juice
of Ivy, oyle of Roſes, and white wine, of each a like
quantity, till it come to a thick ſalve, and then bind
it to the temples of the head, and it will in ſhort
ſpace take away the grief.

For a Dizzinefs in the Head and
to Prevent Apoplectic Fits . . .
Take the ſeedſ and rootſ of ſingle Piony, of each a
like Quantity; dry and beat them feverally into a
fine Powder; take the Weight in Nutmeg, which
you must beat, and dry, and beat again, mix fine
ſifted ſugar, and take aſ much aſ will lie on a ſhil-
ling every Morning for a Month constantly.

For the Head-ach . . .
Take of Roſe-water, of the juice of Camomile,
of woman's milk, of ſtrong wine-vinegar, of each
two spoonfuls, mix them together well up in a
chafing-diſh of coals; then take a piece of dry Roſe-
cake, and ſteep it therein, and as ſoon as it hath
drunk up the liquor, and is thoroughly hot, take a

couple of found Nutmegs, grated to powder, and ftrew them upon the Rofe-cake, then breaking it into two parts, bind it on each fide, upon the temples of the head, fo let the party lye down to reft, and the pain will in a fhort fpace be taken from him.

Another for the Head-ach, and
*   to ftay Bleeding at the Nofe . . .*
Take the white of an Egg, and beat it to oyle; then put to it Rofe-water, and the powder of Alabafter, then take flax and dip it therein, and lay it to the Temples and renew it two or three times a day.

For Frenzy, or Inflammation of
*   the Cauls of the Brain . . .*
Cause the juice of Beets to be with a Syringe squirted up into the patients nostrils, which will purge and cleanfe his head exceedingly; and then give him to drink poffet-ale, in which Violet leaves and Lettuce have been boyled, and it will suddenly bring him to a very temperate mildnefs, and make the paffion of the Frenzy forfake him.

For Sore Eyes, or Blood-fhotten eyes . . .
Take the white of an Egg beaten to oyle, as much Rofe-water, and as much of the juice of Housleek, mix them well together, then dip flax . . . therein,

and lay them upon the ſore eyes, and as they dry,
ſo renew them again, and wet them; and thus do,
till the eyes be well.

For the Pain in the Earſ . . .
Take Oyl of Roſeſ, and a little Vinegar, and put it
to the Ear; then make a Bag of Camomel and Mellilot, and lay it thereunto.

To Deſtroy any Pearl or
    Film in the eye . . .
Take a good handful of Marigold plants, and a
handful of Fennel, as much of May-weed, beat them
together, then ſtrain them with a pint of beer; then
put it into a pot, and ſtop it cloſe, that the ſtrength
may not go out. Then let the offended party, drink
thereof when he is in bed, and lye on that side on
which the Pearl is, and likewise drink of it in the
morning.

A Gargle for a Sore Throat . . .
Take Plantain, and red Roſe-water of Each half a
Pint; the Whiteſ of eggſ beat into Water, 4 ſpoonfulſ, Juice of Housleek, fresh beat, 4 ſpoonfulſ; aſ
much of the Water in which Jewſ-Earſ have been
boil'd; 20 dropſ of vitriol, and an Ounce of Honey
of Roſeſ.

For the Tooth-ach . . .

Take a handful of Daiſy-roote, and waſh them very clean, and dry them with a cloth, and then ſtamp them; and when you have ſtamped them a good while, take the quantity of half a nutshell of bay-salt, and ſtrew it amongſt the roots, and when they are very well beaten, ſtrain them thro' a clean cloth; then grate some Calamus Aromaticus, and mix it good and ſtiff with the juice of the roots, and when you have done so, put it into a quill, and snuff it up into your nose, and you ſhall find eaſe.

A Sure Preſervative for the Tooth-Ach . . .

After having waſhed your mouth with water . . . you ſhould every morning rinse the mouth with a teaſpoonful of Lavender-Water mixed with an equal quantity of warm or cold Water.

To Draw Teeth Without Iron . . .

Take ſome of the green of the Elder-tree, . . . and . . . rub thy teeth & gums, and it will looſen them ſo, as you may take them out.

For a Canker in the Mouth or Gumſ . . .

Mix 40 dropſ of ſpirit of Vitriol, in an Ounce of Honey of Roseſ; keep the ſore Place always moist with this Mixture, and 'tiſ a certain cure.

A Cordial for any Infection at the Heart . . .
Take of Burrage, Langdebeel, and Camomile, of each a good Handful; of Harts-tongue, Red Mint, Violets, and Marygolds, of each half a Handful; boyl them in white-wine, or fair-running water, and boyl them over again well; then ftrain it into an earthen pot, and drink thereof morning and evening, to the quantity of feven fpoonfulf.

An Excellent Poppy-water for an Asthma . . .
Fill a Glaff full of fresh Poppief; pour to it 1 quart of Hyffop water, 1 pint Damafk Rofe Water, 1 pint of Penny-royal Water, and 2 quarts of Compound Briony water; put in also 8 ouncef of fton'd Raisinf, 4 ouncef of flic'd Figf, 2 ouncef of fugar-candy, 2 ouncef of fyrup of Maiden-hair; 2 ouncef of fyrup of Ground Ivy, 2 ouncef of flic'd Licorice, Carraway-feedf, and Aniseed, of each 3 ouncef bruis'd; let these ftand fix weekf in the fun; then ftrain it off; and when the Breath if very bad, drink 4 fpoonfulf: In extremity you may mix half an ounce of Oxymel of fquilf with every Dose.

To Help a Stitch in the Side or Elfewhere . . .
Take Doves-dung, red Rofe-leaves, and put them into a Bag, and quilt it; then thoroughly heat it upon a chafingdifh of coals, with Vinegar in a Plat-

ter; then lay it upon the pained Place, as hot as may be ſuffered, and when it cooleth, heat it again.

For the Hectique Feaver . . .

Take the oyle of Violets, and mix it with a good quantity of the powder of white Poppy-ſeed, . . . and therewith anoint the ſmall and reins of the parties back, evening and morning, . . . and it will not only give eaſe to the Feaver but alſo purge and cleanſe away the dry ſcalings, which is engendered either by this, or any other Feaver whatſoever.

For the Peſtilent Feaver . . .

Cauſe the party firſt to be let blood if his ſtrength will bear it; then you ſhall give him cool Julips made of Endive or Succary Water, or the Syrup of Violets, conferve of Barberries and the juice of Lemmons well-mixed and ſymbolized together.

For a Single Tertian Feaver . . .

Take a quart of Poſſet-ale, the Curd being well drained from the ſame, and put thereunto a good handful of Dandelion; and then ſetting it upon the fire, boyl it till a fourth part be conſumed; then as ſoon as your cold fit beginneth, drink a good Draught thereof, and then either labour till you ſweat, or elſe force yourſelf to ſweat in your bed.

To Make a Pultis to
  Cure any Ague-fore . . .
Take Elder leaves, and feeth them in Milk till they
be foft; then take them up and ftrain them, and
then boyl it again till it be thick; and fo ufe it to
the fore as occafion fhall ferve.

For the Ptisich . . .
Take Hore-hound, Violet-leaves, and Hyffop, of
each a good Handful, feeth them in water and put
thereto a little sugar, Lycoras, and Sugar Candy;
after they have boyled a good while, then ftrain it
into an earthen Vessel, and let the fick drink thereof
fix fpoonfuls at a time morning and evening.

Or . . . take the lungs of a Fox, and lay it in Rofe-
water, or boyl it in Rofe-water; then take it out,
and dry it in fome hot Place without the Sun; then
beat it to powder with Sugar Candy, and eat of this
powder morning and evening.

For a Swelling, Attended with Pain . . .
Chop to Pieces an Ounce of the Roots of Garden
Poppies, and Half an Ounce of Elder Flowers; boyl
then a Quarter of an Hour, in three Pints of Spring
Water, and then ftrain off the Liquour, preffing it
hard out. This is to be ufed as a Fomentation, and
it gives prefent Relief.

For the Violent Pain of the Stone . . .

Make a poffet of Milk and Sack; then take off the Curd, and put a Handful of Cammomile Flowers into the Drink; then put it into a pewter Pot, and let it ftand upon hot Embers, so that it may diffolve, and then drink it as Occafion fhall ferve.

For the Rupture . . .

Take of Daifies, Cumfrey, Polipody of the Oak, of Each a Handful, two Rootf of Ofmund, boyl them in ftrong Ale and Honey, and drink thereof morning, Noone, and night, and it will heal any refonable Rupture.

*To Eafe any Canker or Ulcer,
    and Cleanfe any Wound* . . .

Take a Gallon of running Water, and boyl it to a Pottle; then put to it a Handful of Red Sage, a Handful of Celandine, a Handful of Honey-fucklef, a Handful of Woodbine Leavef and flowers; then take a pennyworth of Grains made into fine Powder, and boyl all very well together; then put to it a Quart of the beft Life-honey of a Year old, and a Pound of Roch-Allom; let all boyl together till it come to a pottle, then ftrain it and pat it into a clofe Vessel, and therewith dreff and anoint the fores as occafion ferves.

A Preſent Remedy for Convulsion Fitſ . . .

Make a Draught of an equal Quantity of Piony, and ſimple black-Cherry Water; and for a man put 30, for a Woman 20, for a Child 5 drops of spirit of Hartſ-horn. Drink thiſ in or before a Fit.

For to Make a Man Sleep,
and for to Come to Quiet Reſt . . .

Take red Roſes, Violets, the Water of Mellilot, of Each a like Quantity, a Handful; white Poppy, white Henbane, of each half a Dram; a little Dill-feet for to comfort the Braine; . . . then put them in a ſoft Linnen Cloth, twelve inches long and three inches broad, quilt it, and tye it to his Fore-head. Alſo take Oyl of Water Lillies, Poppy, Night-ſhade, Roſe-water, Vinegar, and Woman's Milk, dip Flax therein, and bind it to his Temples.

For Melancholy . . .

Conſerve of Marigolds, taken Faſting in the morning, is Good for Melancholy, cureth the trembling and ſhaking of the Heart, is Good to be uſed againſt the Plague, and Corruption of the Aire.

Cosmetic Uses

A Water to Make the Face Fair . . .
Boyl Rofemary Flowerf in white Wine, and wafh your Face with it. This being drank, will make the breath fweet.

A Water of Flowerf,
   Good to Help the Complexion . . .
Take Flowerf of Beanf, Elder, Mallowf, and Flower de Lif, with the Pulp of Melon, Honey, and the White of an Egg; fprinkle them with Wine, let them be infus'd in it for two Dayf, then distil them in *Balneo Marie*.

A Water to Clear the Face from Freckles . . .
Take of Bean Flowerf, and Flowerf de Lif, of each a Pound, of ftrawberries, three Poundf, of fal Geminae and Nitre 4 Drams, of Roche and Plume Allum an Ounce; let all these infuse for a Fortnight, in 2 Quartf of white-Wine Vinegar, the fame Quantity of Malmsey-wine, and af much Hampshire Honey, then distil them in a moderate fandbath; when you go to bed, dip a Rag into this Water, and apply to the Face, Handf, Neck etc., and the next Morning wafh them with Menupharwater.

A Water to Prevent Freckles,
   or Blotchef in the Face . . .

Take wild Cucumber-rootſ and Narciſſus-rootſ, of each an equal Quantity; dry them in the ſhade, and reduce them to a very fine Powder, putting them afterwards into ſtrong French Brandy, with which waſh the Face, till it begins to itch; and then waſh it with cold water. This method muſt be repeated every day till a perfect cure is obtained, which will ſoon happen, for this Water has a ſlight cauſtic Property, and of courſe muſt remove all ſpots on the ſkin.

Pomatum for a Red or Pimpled Face . . .

Take two pared Apples, Celery, and Fennel, of each a Handful; and Barley Meal, a Quarter of an Ounce. Simmer the whole together a Quarter of an Hour in a gill of Roſe-water, then add an Ounce of fine Barley Meal, the whites of four new-large Eggs, and an Ounce of Deer's Suet. Strain through a canvas Bag into a diſh that contains a little Roſe-water; waſh the Pomatum well in the Roſe-water, and afterwards beat it in a Mortar perfectly ſmooth. This Pomatum is to be applied frequently during the day, to remove the redness of the Face, Pimples, and even Freckles.

A Pomatum for Wrinkles . . .

Take Juice of White Lily Roots and fine Honey, of each two Ounces; melted white Wax, an Ounce; incorporate the whole together, and make a pomatum. It ſhould be applied every night, and may not be wiped off till the next Morning.

A Diſtilled Water that Tinges the Cheeks
 a Beautiful Carnation Hue . . .

Take two Quarts of White Wine Vinegar, take three Ounces of Iſinglaſs, two Ounces of bruiſed Nutmegs, and ſix Ounces of Honey; diſtil with a gentle fire, and add to the diſtilled Water a ſmall Quantity of Red Sanders, in order to colour it. Before the Tincture is uſed, a Lady ſhould waſh herſelf with Elder-flower Water, and then the cheeks will become of a fine lively Vermillion, that cannot be diſtinguiſhed from the natural Bloom of Youth.

A Water that Gives a Gloſs to the Skin . . .

Take a Handful of Bean, Elder, and Bugloſs Flowers, a ſmall Pigeon clean drawn, the Juice of two Lemons, four Ounces of Salt, and five Ounces of Camphor; diſtil them in a vapour-bath; add to the diſtilled Water a few grains of Muſk; and expoſe it to the ſun for the ſpace of a month, obſerving to

take the Veſſel within doors every Night. The waye
to uſe this Water, is to dip the corner of a fine Nap-
kin in it, and gently rub the Face.

An Excellent Damaſk Powder . . .
Take of . . . Roſe leaues 4 Ounces, cloues one
Ounce, lignum Rhodium two Ounces, Storax one
Ounce and a half, muſke and ciuet of each 10
graines, beat and incorporate them well together.

A Jonquil Powder . . .
Take 12 lbs and ½ of Starch Powder and ½ lb Jonquil Flowers; ſtrew the Flowers among the Powder,
and at the expiration of twenty Hours, sift it through
a coarſe ſieve. Then throw away the Flowers, and
add to the Powder the ſame Quantity of fresh Flowers. Continue this method 4 or 5 days, obſerving
never to touch the Powder while the Flowers lie
mixed with it; and the former will hence acquire a
very agreeable Perfume.

An Excellent Lip-ſalve . . .
Take an Ounce of Myrrh, as much Litharge in fine
powder, four Ounces of Honey, two Ounces of Bees-
wax, and ſiz Ounces of Oyl of Roſes; mix them
over a ſlow fire.

A Scarlet Lip-falve . . .

Take Hog's Lard wafhed in Rofe-water, half a Pound, Red Rofes and Damafk Rofes bruifed, a quarter of a Pound; knead them together and let them lie in that ftate two days. Then melt the Hog's Lard, and ftrain it from the Rofes. Add a fresh Quantity of the latter, knead them in the Hog's Lard, and let them lie together two days as before; then gently fimmer the mixture in a vapour-bath. Preff out the Lard, and keep it for ufe in the fame manner as other lip-falves.

A Pomatum for the Hair . . .

Cut into fmall pieces of fufficient Quantity of Hog's Cheek, fteep it eight or ten days in clean Water, which be careful to change 3 times a day, and every time the Water is changed, ftir it well with a fpatula to make the Flefh white. Drain the Flefh dry, and putting it into a new earthen Pipkin, with a Pint of Rofe-water, and a Lemon stuck with Cloves, fimmer them over the fire till the fkim looks reddifh. Skim this off, and removing the Pipkin from the fire, ftrain the Liquor. When it has cooled, take off the fat; beat it well with cold Water; which change two or three times as Occafion may require; the laft time ufing Rofe-water, inftead of common

Water. Drain the Pomatum dry, and ſcent it with Violets, Tuberoſes, Orange Flowers, Jasmine, Jonquils, &c, in the following manner: Spread your Pomatum about an Inch thick upon ſeveral diſhes or plates, ſtrewing the Flowers you make choice of on one diſh, and covering them with another. Change the Flowers for freſh ones every 12 Hours, and continue to purſue this method for 10 or 12 days; mixing the Pomatum well, and ſpreading it out every time that freſh Flowers are added. It will ſoon acquire a fragrant ſcent, and may be uſed in what manner you think proper. It is good for almost every coſmetic purpoſe, but particularly for the Hair, which it nouriſhes, ſtrengthens, preſerves, and thickens.

An Excellent Hand-water . . .

Take a Gallon of faire Water, one Handfull of Lauender Flowers, a fewe Cloues, and ſome Orace Powder, and foure Ounces of Benjamin; diſtil the water in an ordinary leaden ſtill.

A Method to Make the Teeth
   Beautifully White . . .

Take Gum Tragacanth, one Ounce; Pumice-ſtone, two Drachms; Gum Arabic, half an Ounce; and Cryſtals of Tartar, finely powdered, one Ounce;

diſſolve the Gums in Roſe-water, and adding to it the Powder, form the whole into little ſticks, which are to be dried ſlowly in the ſhade, and afterwards kept for uſe.

A Conſtant Daily Waſh for Your Teeth . . .
To one Quart of Claret put an Ounce of bole-Armoniack, half an Ounce of Myrrh, 1 Dram of Allom, ſalt of Vitriol ten grains, an ounce of Hungary-water, and 2 ounceſ of honey of Roſes; when these have ſtood in a warm ſun, or near the Fire for 3 Dayſ, set it by to ſettle; and pour a ſpoonful of it into a Tea-cup of Water, with which waſh your Teeth. It preſerves them ſound, and makeſ them white.

General Rules for Cooking with Flowers

1. Select those blossoms, buds, or leaves that are as nearly perfect as possible. Do not use those that have been attacked by any type of plant blight or insect. Do not use flowers that have been sprayed or dusted with insect poisons unless you are certain the insecticide can be washed off.

2. If you are buying flowers from a commercial florist, be sure to ask if any sprays have been used on them and, if so, whether those sprays were water-soluble. If the flowers were subjected to sprays that cannot be rinsed off with water, do *not* use any part of the plant for cooking.

3. Examine flowers carefully for insects. Wash well in cool water and do not bruise petals. Drain thoroughly on paper towels.

4. If you are using buds or blossoms, trim off the stems as closely as possible to the flower.

5. If you are using petals, trim off white tips which attach to stem.

6. Use only glass, enamel, ceramic, or plastic containers for cooking or storing flowers. Use only wooden utensils for stirring.

7. Some flowers may occasionally taste slightly more acrid than usual, depending on their age or the time of year. Compensate for acridity by increasing amount of sugar called for.

8. Not all flowers are edible; in fact, some are highly toxic. Also, some flowers are edible only after they have been subjected to certain preparation processes. Therefore follow preparation instructions precisely. Do *not* substitute other fresh flowers for those recommended in the lists of ingredients. Do *not* experiment with wild flowers unless you are absolutely sure they are not poisonous.

Basic
Flower Cookery Recipes

§ The flower ingredients in this chapter are modernized and simplified versions of recipes taken from cookbooks of the sixteenth, seventeenth, and eighteenth centuries. You will find, as you make your way through this book, that the flower waters, butters, sugars, syrups, honeys, oils, vinegars, and dried petals are used in interesting and diverse ways to complement other food ingredients. This use of preserved flowers and flower derivatives has a long history. Cooks of antiquity discovered that by distilling flower water they could enhance their dishes with the fragrance and flavor of roses even during seasons when roses were not in bloom.

These ingredients were once thought to have truly wondrous properties. For instance, Markham in *The English Hus-wife* (1615) assures his readers that "oyle of Lillies is good to ſupple, mollifie, &

ſtretch ſinews that be ſhrunk," while the anonymous author of *The Toilet of Flora* (1784) suggests that lavender vinegar, "when applied to the face, braces up the relaxed fibres of the ſkin." We cannot vouch for the effectiveness of lavender vinegar and lily oil for facial fibers or shrunken sinews, but we do recommend their use in our recipes for extra taste and fragrance.

NOTE: It is difficult to give exact quantities yielded by the recipes in this section, since so much depends upon the amount of water, the exact number of petals, and the patience of the cook, to mention only a few of the variables. However, since exact quantities will be used later on in the recipes for specific kinds of cookery, this is not a problem.

FLOWER WATER

1 lb. fresh petals, prepared for use	Glass or enamel saucepan with lid
Water	Filter cloth
Glass jar with close-fitting lid	

Wash petals in cold running water and drain. Place about 3 cups of petals in saucepan. Add enough water to cover petals. Cover pan and set over low heat. Let simmer for 40 minutes. Remove petals, and add an equal quantity of fresh petals. Do not add more water. Repeat process until all the petals are used up.

Strain liquid through filter cloth into glass jar, and tighten lid. Store for 2 to 3 days before using.

Makes approximately one pint.

FLOWER BUTTER I

2 cups fresh petals,   Glass or plastic container
     prepared for use   with close-fitting lid
          1 lb. butter

Allow butter to stand at room temperature for 10 to 15 minutes.

Wash petals in cold running water, and drain thoroughly. When petals are dry, spread them in thin layer at bottom of container. Top with a layer of butter (not more than 1 inch thick). Repeat process until petals and butter are used up.

Cover container and tighten lid. Store in refrigerator for about 1 week before using.

(For stronger flavor and fragrance, use more flower petals and thinner layers of butter.)

FLOWER BUTTER II

1 lb. butter
2 tsps. flower water

Glass or plastic container
with close-fitting lid

Allow butter to stand at room temperature for 10 to 15 minutes. Then sprinkle with flower water and beat it in lightly.

Press butter into container, and tighten lid. If not to be used immediately, return to refrigerator.

FLOWER SUGAR

6 cups fresh petals,
prepared for use

Glass or plastic container
with close-fitting lid

3 cups fine granulated sugar

Wash petals in cold runing water. Drain thoroughly on paper towels, and mince.

When petals are no longer wet, pound them together with sugar, using a mortar and pestle, or an electric blender.

Sift flower sugar into the container, cover and tighten lid. Store in warm, dry place for 1 week before using.

FLOWER VINEGAR I

2 cups fresh petals, prepared for use	Glass or enamel saucepan
1 qt. cider vinegar	Glass jar with close-fitting lid
1 cup sugar	
Filter cloth	

Wash petals in cold running water and drain on paper towels.

Pour vinegar into saucepan and set over medium heat. Bring to a boil. Add petals and sugar gradually, stirring constantly.

Bring to boil again. Then lower heat, and let simmer for 10 minutes.

Strain liquid through filter cloth into glass jar. Tighten lid, and store in warm place for 1 week before using.

POWDERED FLOWER PETALS

3 cups dried petals	Glass jar with close-fitting lid
Flour sifter	

Pulverize dried petals, using mortar and pestle. Then, using a flour sifter, sift petals into glass jar. Tighten lid, and store in warm, dry place.

FLOWER VINEGAR II

2 cups dried petals   Stone or crockery jar
Distilled vinegar   with close-fitting lid

Set petals in jar, and add enough vinegar to cover petals. Cover jar, and set in warm place for at least 1 week. Strain liquid through filter cloth into any glass container. Filtered liquid may be used immediately, or stored in cool place.

DISTILLED FLOWER WATER

1 lb. fresh flower petals,   Pan of cold water
   prepared for use   Rubber tubing
Water   (approximately 4 ft.)
Enamel teakettle with   Glass jar with
   close-fitting lid   close-fitting lid

Fill teakettle with water to halfway mark, and set over low heat. Ease one end of rubber tubing over spout (tubing should fit tightly), and place other end in glass container. Allow middle section of tubing to rest in pan of cold water. Fill teakettle with petals, stir, and cover. As petals boil down, add more petals until all are used. Steam from spout will enter tubing and condense at point where tubing passes through cold water. Distilled flower water will then drip into glass container at other end.

When water has ceased dripping into glass container, cover it tightly and store for 2 to 3 days before using.

Distilled flower water has a stronger flavor and fragrance than ordinary flower water. Use only half as much as recipe calls for.

DRIED FLOWER PETALS

3 cups fresh petals,   Wire window screen
  prepared for use   on frame
     Glass container with close-fitting lid

Wash petals in cold running water, and drain thoroughly.

Spread them over a cloth-covered window screen. Be sure no petal touches another. Cover petals with cheesecloth, and set aside to dry.

Petals will dry quickly if put outdoors in the shade. But they will retain a stronger color and fragrance if allowed to dry more slowly in a warm, dry place, out of reach of sunlight or direct heat.

When petals are thoroughly dried, place them in container and tighten lid. Store in warm, dry place.

FLOWER SYRUP I

4 cups dried petals
Water
Glass or enamel sauce-
    pan

Sugar
Glass container with
    close-fitting lid
Filter cloth

Place dried petals in pan, and press down. Add enough cold water to cover petals, one measured cup at a time, keeping count.

Bring to boil. Then lower heat and gradually add sugar (3 cups for every cup of water used). Bring to boil again. Then lower flame and keep at just under a boil until syrup forms (10 to 12 minutes).

Strain through filter cloth into glass jar. Cover tightly, and store in warm place for at least 10 days before using.

FLOWER SYRUP II

4 cups fresh petals,
    prepared for use
Water
Filter cloth
Paper towels

Glass or enamel sauce-
    pan
Sugar
Glass jar with
    close-fitting lid

Wash petals in cold running water, and drain. Place petals in glass jar, and add enough boiling water to cover. Cool for 5 minutes, then cover and tighten lid on jar, and set aside for 48 hours.

Then strain flower mixture through filter cloth. Measure filtered liquid. Pour into saucepan and for each cup of liquid add 2 cups of sugar. Bring to boil. Lower heat, and let simmer until syrup forms (10 to 12 minutes).

Pour syrup into glass jar, and tighten lid. Store in warm place for at least 1 week before using.

FLOWER OIL

3 cups fresh petals,   Glass jar with
  prepared for use   close-fitting lid
        1 qt. salad oil

Wash petals in cold running water, and drain thoroughly on paper towels. When petals are no longer wet, mince them.

Pour oil into jar, and add minced petals. Set jar in a pan of water, set over low heat, and allow to simmer gently for 30 minutes.

Then remove jar from pan, cover tightly, and wrap in towel. Store in warm place for at least 10 days. Strain before using.

FLOWER HONEY

1 cup fresh petals, prepared for use	Glass or enamel saucepan
1 pt. honey	Glass jar with close-fitting lid
Paper towels	

Wash petals in cold running water, and drain on paper towels.

When petals are no longer wet, pour honey into saucepan and set over medium heat. Bring to a boil, lower heat, and add petals. Let simmer for 10 minutes, then remove from heat. Set aside, at room temperature, for 24 hours.

Set over medium heat again and bring to a boil. Remove from heat and strain into glass jar. Tighten lid, and store in warm place for 2 to 3 days before using.

PICKLED FLOWER BUDS

½ lb. fresh buds, prepared for use	½ lb. fine granulated sugar
Glass or plastic container with close-fitting lid	Distilled vinegar (approximately 1 qt.)

Glass or enamel saucepan

Wash buds in cold running water, and drain. Cover the bottom of container with a layer of buds, and cover buds with a layer of sugar. Repeat process until both buds and sugar are used up.

Bring vinegar to a boil in saucepan, over medium heat. Pour vinegar over buds until it just covers them.

Tighten lid on container, and store in warm place for at least 10 days before using.

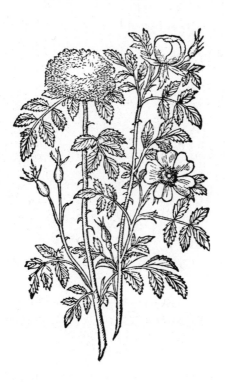

Flower Beverages

§ Beverages of all kinds were once brightened by flower ingredients. Today we are most intrigued, perhaps, with the Englishman's way with flower spirits. Dandelions, marigolds, elder flowers, carnations, violets, primroses, and many other blossoms were plucked by English householders, added to other ingredients, then allowed to "work" until ready to be bottled for what one cookbook author termed "cordial, wholesome and pleasant consumption."

The dandelion wine described in this chapter was a favorite of wine connoisseurs of long ago. Among the brandies, orange-blossom brandy, represented here, was especially popular. Our recipes are translated, of course, into modern terms—with modern ingredients. For a look back at the antique wine and brandy recipes, we point with awe to one calling for 400 cracked apricot stones. John Nott (in

The Cook's and Confectioner's Dictionary, 1723)
was the original bottler of the following hearty
beverage

"To a gallon of Brandy, add a quart of French
white wine and a quart of orange flower water, and
400 apricot ſtones crack'd, and a pound and a quarter of fine Sugar, put them into a large bottle, ſtop
it cloſe, ſeal it down, and set it in the Sun for 6
weeks, taking it in every Night, if it be wet weather,
and ſhake it twice a Day; then let it ſtand to settle,
and rack it off till it is thoroughly fine."

F L O W E R   T E A S

1 tsp. dried leaves for	*or* 3 tsps. of
each cup of tea desired	fresh leaves
plus 1 tsp. for the pot,	Boiling water

Use dried flowers of camomile, dried or fresh
leaves and flower buds of lavender, dried or fresh
leaves of geranium, dried or fresh rose petals, dried
leaves of sweet goldenrod.

If you are using fresh leaves, bruise them gently
first by crushing carefully in a clean cloth.

Use boiling water to rinse and warm the teapot.
Add dried leaves or bruised fresh ones to pot. Pour
boiling water over leaves, and steep 3 to 5 minutes
only before serving.

ROSE-GERANIUM TEA

English tea leaves	1 leaf of rose geranuim
(1 tsp. for each cup	2 cloves
and 1 for the teapot)	½ stick cinnamon
Boiling water	

Place the tea leaves, rose-geranium leaf, cloves, and cinnamon stick in the teapot. Pour boiling water into the pot. Infuse 3 to 5 minutes, and serve.

LIME-GERANIUM LEMONADE

Juice of 4 lemons	6 small sprigs or
6 cups cold water	6 large leaves
6 tsps. sugar	of lime geranium
6 strips of lime peel	

Strain the lemon juice into the water; add 3 teaspoonfuls of sugar.

In each glass crush 1 lime-geranium sprig with ½ teaspoon sugar. Use the back of a wooden spoon for this.

Test for sweetness. Add more sugar if necessary. Pour lemonade into glasses. Add crushed ice and garnish each with a twist of lime peel.

LAVENDER-PINEAPPLE DRINK

1 pineapple	Juice of 2 lemons,
½ lb. sugar	strained
3 pts. water	A few lavender petals

Slice the pineapple, then cut into small cubes or chop coarsely.

Boil the sugar and 1 pint of water until the sugar is completely dissolved.

Pour the syrup over the prepared pineapple. Add the lemon juice to this mixture. Cover tightly and chill.

When the pineapple drink is quite cold, add 2 pints of cold water, float the lavender petals in the beverage and serve.

FESTIVE WINE CUP WITH BORAGE

2 lemons	¼ lb. granulated sugar
Few cubes sugar	1½ pts. water
Few leaves lemon balm	½ bottle Madeira
2 or 3 sprigs of borage	¼ pt. French brandy
1 bottle champagne	

Rub the skin of 1 lemon with a few sugar cubes, then peel and remove every particle of white pulp. Remove peel and pulp of other lemon with a scraper. Slice lemons thinly.

Place the balm, borage, sliced lemons, and all the sugar in a large 3-quart pitcher. Add the water, Madeira, and brandy. Cover, surround with ice, and let the mixture stand for approximately 1 hour.

Meanwhile, surround the champagne with ice. Add it to the rest of the ingredients just before serving.

EGGNOG À LA ROSE

2 eggs, separated
2½ Tbs. rose syrup
   (p. 32)

1 cup cream
1 cup milk
Mace

Beat the egg yolks, then pour in rose syrup, cream, and milk. Beat well. Whip the egg whites until stiff but not dry, and fold them into the egg-yolk mixture. Sprinkle lightly with mace and serve.

ORANGE-FLOWER BRANDY

½ lb. orange blossoms,
2 cups water

½ gal. French brandy
½ cup sugar

Boil the orange blossoms for 30 minutes in water to cover (approximately 2 cups). Strain, reserving the liquid in which the flowers were cooked. Then add orange flowers to the brandy.

Dissolve sugar in the reserved orange-flower water. Bring to the boil, allow to boil for a few minutes until the syrup is slightly thickened. Add the syrup to the brandy, mix, and cover tightly.

S U M M E R   R E F R E S H E R

Pilsener beer, chilled   Honey-locust pods

Float honey-locust pods in cold glass of Pilsener beer for summertime refreshment.

M A Y   B O W L

2 bottles Moselle wine   1 pint strawberries,
1 bunch woodruff,   hulled and cleaned
   washed   2 oranges, peeled
½ cup sugar   and cut in slices
1 cup water   1 bottle seltzer water
                    Cracked ice

Combine wine and woodruff in a bowl. Cover tightly and pack bowl in a second bowl or other container filled with ice. Let stand for 30 minutes.

Meanwhile, melt the sugar in the water.

When the 30 minutes are up, remove the woodruff and mix the sugar water with the wine.

Add the strawberries and orange slices. Just before serving, add the seltzer water.

DANDELION WINE

4 qts. dandelion flowers	1-in. piece of
4 qts. boiling water	whole candied ginger
Rind of 1 orange	½ cake yeast moistened
1 lemon	with 1 Tbs. water
3 lbs. granulated sugar	1 piece of toast

Place the petals of the dandelions in a large 6-quart bowl. Pour the boiling water over them. Cover the bowl and allow to stand 3 days, stirring frequently.

Strain the liquid into a large kettle. Add the rinds of the orange and lemon (both should be pared off in thin, fine strips). Also add the sugar, ginger, and the lemon which has been cut in thin slices.

Boil this mixture gently for about ½ hour.

Meanwhile, spread the moistened yeast on a piece of toast. Add toast to liquid.

Place liquid in preserving crock, cover with cheesecloth and allow to stand in a warm room 5 days.

Strain the liquid into a gallon jug. Cork it loosely with a wad of cotton. Keep in a dark place for 4 weeks. Then bottle the wine and cork tightly. Keep for several months before using.

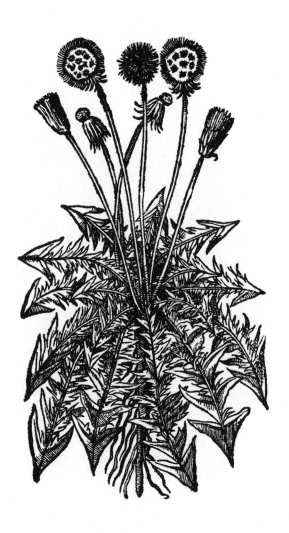

Flower Canapés

§ We tend to think of canapés as inventions as new
as the extra-dry martini and designed to be eaten
only at cocktail time. Actually, many kinds of
canapés are simply particular versions of dishes that
have long since been associated with more traditional repasts—and even with the conservative tea-
table of Victorian times.

From E. Smith's *The Compleat Housewife*
(1727) comes the inspiration for our Orange-
flower Meat Balls. She suggests that you mince the
meat "very fine, then chop a few herbs, & put to it
. . . a little Salt, . . . some yolks of Eggs, & a
handfull of grated bread, . . . & Orange-Flower
Water. . . ."

The recipes for Flowered Eggplant and Laven-
der-Caviar Dip were given to us by friends. Their
origins are shrouded in the mists of family history,
but they are as delicious as any of the others.

ORANGE-FLOWER MEAT BALLS

1 egg   1 tsp. fennel seeds
1 lb. lean ground pork   1 cup orange-flower oil
1 tsp. salt   (p. 33)

Beat egg lightly, and blend with ground meat in large bowl. Add salt and fennel seeds and mix together thoroughly. Shape into bite-sized balls, about one inch in diameter.

Heat oil in skillet and deep-fry meat balls. Serve hot, on toothpicks. Serves 6 to 8.

MARIGOLD CHEESE BALLS

8 slices white bread   1½ tsps. powdered
¼ cup marigold butter   marigold petals
1 garlic clove   (p. 29)
4 egg whites   ¾ tsp. baking powder
½ tsp. salt

1 cup grated Cheddar cheese

Trim crusts off bread slices. Cut slices into small squares or circles (about 4 to the slice).

Heat butter in skillet, and sauté garlic. When garlic turns deep gold, discard it. Sauté bread squares, on one side only, until they turn a delicate brown. Drain on paper towels.

In a large bowl, beat egg whites until they peak. Gradually add powdered petals, salt, and baking powder, beating constantly. Gradually add cheese, and beat until thoroughly blended.

Spoon cheese mixture onto unbrowned side of bread square. Place cheese squares 4 to 5 inches beneath broiler, and broil until top of cheese turns light brown.

Serve immediately.

Serves 6.

ROSE-CREAM CHEESE TIDBITS

1 pkg. cream cheese
(3 oz.)
2 Tbs. cream
1½ tsps. powdered rose petals (p. 29)

1 tsp. chives
1 tsp. sugar
½ cup fresh rose petals, prepared for use
Toasted wheat thins

Allow cream cheese to stand at room temperature for 10 minutes. Then, in a large mixing bowl, combine cream cheese, cream, powdered petals, chives, and sugar. Blend together thoroughly with spoon. Chill for 30 minutes.

Spread cream-cheese mixture on wheat thins, top with rose petals, and serve.

Serves 6 to 8.

FLOWERED EGGPLANT CANAPÉS

1 medium eggplant
1 cup primrose oil
   (p. 33)
½ cup onion, chopped
3 celery stalks, chopped
1 minced garlic clove
2 cups tomato purée
1 Tbs. salt
1 bay leaf
¼ cup capers
1 doz. green olives,
   pitted and sliced
¼ cup vinegar
¼ cup sugar
Rye or whole wheat
   thins

Cheese

Wash eggplant and cut, unpeeled, into ¾-inch cubes. Soak in salted water 20 minutes, then drain thoroughly.

Reserve 3 tablespoons of oil and heat remainder in large skillet. Sauté onion until golden, and drain on paper towels. Next, in same oil, fry eggplant, and drain on paper towels. Next, fry celery until tender, and drain.

While vegetables are draining, wipe skillet clean. Heat reserved 3 tablespoons oil in cleaned skillet, and sauté garlic. When garlic turns golden, add tomato, salt, and bay leaf. Let simmer, covered, for 25 minutes, stirring occasionally.

Add drained vegetables, capers, olives, vinegar, and sugar. Mix thoroughly and let simmer, covered, for 30 minutes, stirring occasionally.

Serve hot, or thoroughly chilled, on rye or whole wheat thins which have ben topped with small slices of bland cheese.

Serves 8 to 10.

LAVENDER-CAVIAR DIP

2 slices white bread
¼ cup lemon juice
2 cups red caviar
1 minced garlic clove

½ cup lavender oil
2 Tbs. shredded fresh
   lavender petals,
   prepared for use

Thins or unsalted crackers

Trim crust from bread slices, and moisten slices with lemon juice. Blend together bread, remaining lemon juice, caviar, and garlic. Add lavender oil gradually, beating constantly until mixture is smooth and completely blended.

Place caviar in serving dish, and garnish with shredded petals. Serve with toasted thins or unsalted crackers.

Serves 8 to 10.

Flower Soups

§ Elizabeth Cleland's idea for a delectable soup was a pottage concocted out of spinach, marigold flowers, strawberry leaves, violet leaves, and miscellaneous ingredients. In *A New and Easy Method of Cookery* (second edition, 1759), she directed eighteenth-century housewives in their preparation of this pottage as follows: First, "mince Spinage, Chives, Parsley, Marigold Flowers, Succory, Strawberry and Violet leaves. Then ſtamp them with oatmeal." She added, "You may either put Broth or water to them."

This pottage is typical of one type of soup that has come down to us from earlier centuries—the soup or chowder combining flower petals, flower leaves, fruit, or roots with unusual ingredients. In this chapter we have adapted several of these recipes calling for interesting combinations of flowers with vegetables and herbs. You will find marigold petals with potatoes, onion and celery; dandelions with chives; violet rootstocks with parsley, and daylilies with turnip and a grand assortment of vegetables and herbs.

Hannah Glasse in her famous *Art of Cookery Made Plain and Easy* (1747), turns a turnip, dried marigold flowers, and a mutton scrag into a zestful mutton broth:

"Take a 6-pound neck of mutton, cut in two. Boil scrag in a gallon of water and skim. Put in a bundle of ſweet herbs, onion, and cruſt of bread. Let boil 1 hour, add the reſt of the mutton. A quarter hour before the end, add 1 turnip, dried marigold flowers, chopped chives and parſley. Add salt."

DAYLILY SOUP

1 Tbs. butter	Bouquet garni fresh or
½ Medium-size onion, sliced	dried herbs—1 tsp. parsley, ½ tsp. thyme, bay leaf)
½ carrot, sliced	
¼ yellow turnip, sliced	3 peppercorns
2 qts. water	½ tsp. salt
1 lb. shin of beef, cut into small pieces	1 Tbs. flour
	½ cup daylily buds

Heat the butter in a large saucepan. Add the sliced onion, carrot, and turnip, and brown.

Next, add the water, meat, bouquet garni, peppercorns, and salt. Simmer slowly for approximately 3 to 4 hours. Strain. Cool, skim off fat, then reheat.

Mix flour with a small amount of cold water and stir in carefully. Gently boil soup for 10 minutes, adding daylily buds during the last 5 minutes. Serve, leaving in the daylily buds for garnish and flavor.

POTTAGE OF VIOLETS

1 cup cooked violet rootstocks, chopped fine	1 tsp. salt
	¼ tsp. pepper
	2 Tbs. butter
1 tsp. minced parsley	2 Tbs. flour
1½ cups chicken stock	2 cups milk

Rootstocks should be trimmed and cleaned well, then cooked in water to cover for 20 minutes.

Put violet rootstocks together with the parsley in chicken stock and cook for 25 minutes. Add milk and season with salt and pepper. Bring to the boiling point. Cream butter and flour together and stir into soup. Cook slowly until soup is slightly thickened. Strain if desired.

DANDELION SOUP

2 Tbs. butter

2 Tbs. flour

2 cups milk, boiling

½ tsp. salt

¼ tsp. pepper

2 cups chopped
 dandelion leaves

1 Tbs. chopped parsley

2 tsps. chopped chives

Melt butter in a heavy saucepan. Add flour and stir with a wire whisk until perfectly blended. Remove from heat and add all boiling milk, stirring in carefully. Heat to boiling point and boil 1 minute. Season with salt and pepper.

Press dandelion leaves through a sieve and add to white sauce, stirring constantly; reheat if necessary. Garnish with chopped parsley and chives.

ALMOND ROSE SOUP

2 cups rose hips
 (fruit of roses)

2 qts. water

¼ tsp. salt

Dash pepper

⅓ cup sugar

¼ tsp. almond extract

2 Tbs. flour mixed
 with 1 Tbs. water

½ cup claret

Whipped cream

Slivered almonds

Prepare the rose hips by boiling them with salt and pepper in 2 quarts water. (NOTE: If dried hips are used, soak them overnight and boil them in the same water that was used for soaking.) When the hips are soft, pass them through a sieve to remove skins and seeds. Add sugar and almond extract to the mixture; add flour paste, stirring constantly. Cook until thickened slightly.

Just before serving, add the claret and garnish with whipped cream topped with slivered almonds.

GOLDEN BROTH

2-lb chicken, cut in small pieces	½ cup uncooked soup noodles
1 qt. cold water	¼ tsp. pulverized pot marigold (p. 29)
1 tsp. salt	

Combine chicken and water in heavy saucepan. Cook for 2 hours. Then add salt and stir well. Strain broth, and chill until fat rises to the top. Skim off fat carefully.

Cook soup noodles until barely done. Drain and add to broth along with pulverized marigold.

MARIGOLD CHOWDER

6 medium-size potatoes	Salt
1 large onion	2 cups water
2 Tbs. butter	1 qt. milk plus 1 Tbs.
1 cup chopped celery	1 Tbs. flour
1 Tbs. chopped parsley	¼ cup marigold petals

Peel potatoes and cut into small pieces.

Chop the onion. Heat the butter in a frying pan until it foams, then add the onion and brown lightly.

Place a layer of potatoes in the bottom of a kettle, then a layer of celery plus a little of the parsley, a dash of salt, and some of the onion. Continue in this manner until all the vegetables are used. Add water and simmer, covered, 20 minutes without stirring.

Add 1 quart milk and heat the mixture, but do not let it boil. Moisten the flour and ¼ teaspoon salt with 1 tablespoon of cold milk. Stir this flour paste into the soup mixture along with the marigold petals. Heat slowly until soup reaches boiling point, stirring constantly.

Flowered Egg Dishes

§ Egg dishes have always been popular, perhaps because eggs were an adequate substitute at times when meat was either too expensive or not easily available. One of the recipes adapted for this chapter is the "Omelet called Quelchecho*f*e," which, reports Markham in *The English Hus-wife*, is a Continental concoction, "a mixture of many things together. . . . Take the Eggs and break them, and do away one half of the Whites, and after they are beaten, put them to a good quantity of *f*weet Cream, Currants, Cinamon, Cloves, Mace, Salt, and a little Ginger, Spinage, Endive, and Mary-gold flowers, and beat them all together; then take . . . Petti-toes flic'd and gro*f*ly chopt, mix them with the Eggs. . . . Fry in *f*weet Butter . . ."

Although modern housewives regard the soufflé as a culinary miracle of hairbreadth measurements and split-second timing, early-nineteenth-century cooks were far more casual about both. Our Orange-Flower Soufflé, for example, was adapted from Louis Eustache Ude in *The French Cook* (1813), who says only, "Dilute a little flour with half cream & milk; set this pap on the fire to boil; when the flour is done, put a little salt, a little sugar, & a small quantity of pounded orange flower, mix well, & then add a good bit of butter, the yolks of six eggs, & mix the whole well. Next beat the Six whites & mix them with the rest; then . . . put it into the oven, which must not be too hot, and when it is baked enough, glaze it, powder a little Sugar over it, & send it up."

You may try this one, if you're feeling adventuresome, but ours tastes just as good and the recipe is lots easier to follow.

ROSE-DEVILED EGGS

8 hard-boiled eggs	1 tsp. salt
2 Tbs. mayonnaise	1 tsp. sugar
1 Tbs. lemon juice	¼ tsp. black pepper
1 tsp. powdered rose petals (p. 29)	¼ cup shredded fresh rose petals, prepared for use
1 tsp. grated onion	

Shell eggs, and cut in half lengthwise. Carefully scoop out the yolks, and set the white aside.

Mash the yolks in a mixing bowl. Add mayonnaise, lemon juice, powdered petals, onion, salt, sugar, and pepper. Stir slowly to blend, then beat until mixture is fluffy.

Spoon mixture into egg whites. Or, for a more attractive effect, force mixture through a paper cone and fill egg white in squirls. Set filled whites on serving platter, and garnish with shredded petals.

SHIRRED TULIP EGGS

6 tulip blossoms, prepared for use	2 Tbs. butter
	⅓ cup cream
6 eggs	1 tsp. salt
Dash of black pepper	

Preheat over to 350° F.

Wash blossoms carefully under cold, running water, and drain on paper towels.

Break each egg into greased individual baking dish. Dot each egg with butter, add a scant tablespoon of cream, and sprinkle with salt and pepper. Bake until eggs are set (about 15 minutes).

When eggs are done, spread petals of tulip blossoms and slide egg into flower. Arrange filled blossoms on serving platter.

Serve immediately.

ORANGE-FLOWER SOUFFLÉ

½ lb. mushrooms
3 eggs, separated
¼ cup orange-flower butter (p. 28)
¼ cup flour
1 cup milk
1 tsp. orange-flower water (p. 26)

1 tsp. powdered orange-flower petals (p. 29)
1 Tbs. shredded fresh orange-flower petals, prepared for use
½ tsp. salt
¼ tsp. black pepper

Greased baking dish

Preheat over to 325°F.

Clean mushrooms, and trim off tough ends of stems. Chop mushrooms fine, and let drain thoroughly.

Beat egg yolks until light and frothy, and set aside.

Heat butter in skillet, and sauté mushrooms. When mushrooms are lightly browned, gradually add flour, stirring constantly. After flour is thoroughly blended in, gradually add milk, orange-flower water, powdered and fresh petals, and salt and pepper, still stirring constantly. Add the beaten egg yolks, and stir 1 minute longer. Remove mixture from heat and let cool.

While mixture is cooling, beat egg whites until they peak. Fold egg whites into cooled mixture. Pour into greased baking dish, and set dish in pan of hot water. Bake until soufflé is firm (about 45 minutes).

Serve immediately.

QUELCHE CHOSE OMELET

6 eggs	½ tsp. mace
2 Tbs. light cream	½ tsp. cinnamon
3 Tbs. marigold petals, prepared for use	1 tsp. salt
	½ tsp. pepper
1 tsp. marigold water	2 Tbs. butter
1 cup cooked potatoes, cubed	

Beat eggs until frothy, and add cream, marigold petals, marigold water, mace, cinnamon, salt, and pepper.

Melt butter in skillet, and sauté potatoes. When potatoes are golden, add egg mixture. Cook over low heat, stirring constantly to keep omelet from sticking.

When underside is golden brown, fold omelet in half and slide onto serving dish.

CARNATION-EGG PATTIES

1 cup bread crumbs
2 Tbs. grated Parmesan
   cheese
1 Tbs. chopped parsley
1 tsp. powdered carna-
   tion petals (p. 29)

1 tsp. salt
Dash of garlic powder
4 eggs
4 Tbs. carnation butter
   (p. 28)
   Water

In a large mixing bowl, combine bread crumbs, grated cheese, parsley, powdered petals, salt, and garlic powder. Mix together thoroughly.

Beat eggs until they are light and frothy, and stir them into the dry ingredients, to form wet paste.

Heat butter in skillet. Using your fingers, roll egg mixture into patties. Use a few drops of cold water, if necessary, to help patty hold shape, and ease each into skillet. Sauté over low heat until patties are golden-brown on underside, then carefully turn them over to brown on other side.

FLOWER-JELLY OMELET

4 eggs
4 Tbs. cream
½ tsp. salt

2 Tbs. butter
½ cup flower jelly
   (p. 157)
¼ tsp. black pepper

Beat eggs until light and frothy. Add cream, salt, and pepper, and beat vigorously 2 minutes longer.

Heat butter in skillet over low heat, and pour in beaten eggs. As underside of omelet sets and turns pale golden brown, lift sides of omelet with flat utensil so that uncooked portion will drip down and cook.

As soon as omelet is set, spread jelly on top, fold omelet in half, and slide out onto serving platter.

Serve immediately.

POACHED ORANGE-FLOWER EGGS

Water

1 Tbs. vinegar

1 tsp. salt

1 tsp. orange-flower water (p. 26)

2 Tbs. sugar

2 Tbs. orange-flower petals, prepared for use

1 tsp. lemon juice

1 seedless orange, peeled and sliced

6 eggs

Put 1–1¼ inches of water into a skillet. Add vinegar, salt, and orange-flower water, and set over medium heat. Add sugar gradually, stirring constantly until sugar melts and forms a light syrup. Bring to a boil and immediately lower heat.

Drop eggs into syrup, one at a time, and cook until white is firm. Arrange cooked eggs on serving platter.

Drop flower petals into syrup. Bring to a boil, and remove from heat. Drain petals, and sprinkle over eggs. Sprinkle eggs with lemon juice, surround with orange slices, and serve.

ROSE CHEESE FONDUE

1 cup milk	½ tsp. salt
3 eggs, separated	1 tsp. rose water
1 cup bread crumbs	1¼ cups grated
2 Tbs. rose butter	sharp Cheddar cheese
(or plain butter)	Candied rose petals

Warm milk in top half of double boiler. Beat egg yolks lightly and add to milk, together with bread crumbs, butter, salt, and rose water. Stir constantly, over low flame, until thickened. Stir in grated cheese.

Remove mixture from stove and allow to cool to room temperature.

Preheat oven to 325° F.

Beat egg whites until they peak, and fold carefully into the cheese mixture. Pour into greased baking dish, and bake 55 minutes, or until firm.

Top with candied rose petals, if desired, and return to oven for 5 minutes more. Serve immediately.

Flower Salads

§ Our forebears seem to have had a great deal of time to spend in the kitchen, and so they could indulge their fondness for complicated dishes. "To make a grand Sallet for the Spring," suggests John Nott in *The Cook's and Confectioner's Dictionary* (1723), "take cowſlip buds, violet flowers and leaves, young lettuce, ſpinage, Alexander buds, Strawberry-leaves, water-creſſes, Brooklime. . . . Also take capers, olives, camphire, cucumers, broom-buds, raiſins, and currants parboil'd, almonds blanch'd. . . . Then lay a turnip . . . in the middle of the Sallet, let it be formed like a caſtle made of paſte, waſhed over with the yolk of eggs, & within it a tree made in like manner & covered with green herbs & ſtuck with flowers. . . . Then having made 4 rings of Paſte, each bigger than the other, the big-geſt muſt compass the caſtle & reach within 3 inches of the Feet . . . & so place as many as you think convenient . . . like so many *f*teps one above another, then place 1 sort of your Sallet round on the uppermo*f*t Rings, & so on . . . ; then garni*f*h your Di*f*h with all things *f*uitable to the Season. . . ." But table tastes have changed over the past two hundred years, and so has the schedule of the modern housewife. We've kept most of John Nott's ingredients, but we've put them together in a simpler and easier dish. He'd recognize the name. It's "Spring Salad."

S P R I N G   S A L A D

1 head lettuce, shredded
1 large salad bowl
1 cup violet leaves and petals, prepared for use
½ cup pickled cowslip buds (p. 34)
1 large cucumber, peeled and sliced
½ cup green olives, pitted and halved
¼ cup slivered almonds
4 Tbs. olive oil
2 Tbs. violet vinegar (p. 29 or 30)
½ tsp. salt
Pepper to taste
2–3 sprigs fresh mint

Wash lettuce, flower petals and leaves in cold running water, and drain. Place in a large salad bowl. Add cowslip buds, cucumber, olives, and almonds.

Combine oil, vinegar, salt, and pepper. Pour mixture over salad. Toss lightly, and chill for at least 30 minutes.

Before serving, garnish with fresh mint sprigs.

VIOLET-PERIWINKLE SALAD

1 head escarole	3 Tbs. olive oil
1 head Romaine lettuce	1 Tbs. violet vinegar
½ cup violet leaves, prepared for use	1 tsp. salt
	½ tsp. black pepper

10 periwinkle blossoms, prepared for use

Wash greens, flowers and leaves under cold running water. Drain thoroughly on paper towels.

Shred lettuce and escarole into large bowl. Arrange violet leaves in circle on top of greens, and fill in center of circle with blossoms. Chill for at least 45 minutes.

Combine oil, vinegar, salt, and pepper. Sprinkle dressing over salad, just before serving, but do not toss until salad is on table.

PLUM-BLOSSOM POTATO SALAD

6 medium potatoes	1 Tbs. minced parsley
¼ cup olive oil	1 tsp. salt
3 Tbs. lemon juice	½ tsp. black pepper
1 small green onion, chopped	1 cup pickled plum-blossom buds, drained
1 large bowl	(p. 34)

Boil potatoes, unpeeled, in salted water to cover, until tender. Then drain, peel, and dice. Place the potatoes in a large bowl.

Combine the oil, lemon juice, onion, parsley, salt, and pepper. Pour mixture over potatoes. Add pickled buds, and toss lightly.

Chill for at least 30 minutes before serving.

NASTURTIUM SALAD

4 cups nasturtium blossoms	1 garlic clove
½ cup violet leaves	½ tsp. salt
2 Tbs. chopped chervil leaves	½ tsp. black pepper
	2 Tbs. lemon juice
	3 Tbs. olive oil

Trim off and discard nasturtium leaves and stems. Wash blossoms and violet leaves carefully under cold running water. Drain on paper towels.

Rub inside of wooden salad bowl with garlic clove. Place blossoms in bowl, and add violet leaves, chervil, salt, and pepper. Sprinkle with lemon juice and oil. Toss lightly, and serve immediately.

WILTED DANDELION SALAD

3 cups dandelion leaves	2	Tbs. vinegar
5 strips bacon	1	Tbs. sugar
Salt and pepper to taste		

Wash dandelion leaves in cold running water, and drain. Place in salad bowl.

Cook bacon in skillet over low heat until crisp. Drain on paper towels, and cut into 1-inch pieces.

Pour out all but approximately 2 tablespoons of bacon fat from skillet. Add vinegar and sugar to remaining fat, and stir until blended.

Pour mixture over dandelion leaves. Add bacon, and season with salt and pepper. Toss lightly, and serve.

TULIP-CRABMEAT SALAD

1 doz. tulip blossoms,
prepared for use
1 cup canned crabmeat

2 Tbs. capers
2 Tbs. mayonnaise
2 Tbs. minced parsley

Wash tulip blossoms carefully under cold running water, and drain on paper towels.

In a large bowl, combine crabmeat, capers, and mayonnaise. Mix together thoroughly.

To fill tulips, hold a blossom in palm of hand and with the other hand carefully spoon crabmeat mixture into blossoms. Arrange filled blossoms on serving platter and garnish with parsley.

FLOWER-FRUIT MOLDED SALAD

1 Tbs. unflavored
gelatin
½ cup cold water
1 cup hot water
¼ cup lemon juice
2 Tbs. sugar
½ tsp. salt

3 small marigold
blossoms, prepared
for use
6 small rose blossoms,
prepared for use
1 cup peeled apple
cubes

1 cup sliced bananas

Dissolve gelatin in cold water, and add hot water. Stir in lemon juice, sugar, and salt. Chill until gelatin begins to thicken and become syrupy.

Rinse mold in cold water, and pour in one third of gelatin mixture. Arrange marigold blossoms, face down, in cluster in bottom center of mold. Arrange rose blossoms, face down, in circle around marigolds. When mixture has set, pour in half of remaining mixture. Fold in apple cubes next. When that has set, pour in rest of mixture. Add banana slices. Chill until firm.

Unmold on large lettuce leaves, and serve.

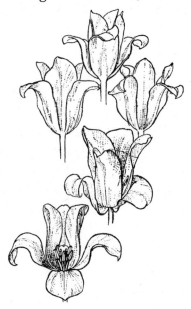

FRAGRANT TOMATO SALAD

4 medium tomatoes	½ tsp. salt
3 Tbs. rose oil	½ tsp. powdered rose
1 Tbs. rose vinegar	petals (p. 29)
(p. 29 or 30)	6 fresh basil leaves

Wash tomatoes and wipe dry. Cut vertically into thin wedges and arrange on serving platter.

Combine oil, vinegar, salt, and powdered petals, and sprinkle mixture over tomatoes. Garnish with basil leaves and serve.

ROSE-CHRYSANTHEMUM SALAD

1 cup white chrysanthemum petals, prepared for use	1 cup rose petals, prepared for use
1 cup yellow chrysanthemum petals, prepared for use	2 cups violet leaves, prepared for use
	3 Tbs. olive oil
	1 Tbs. vinegar
	1 Tbs. sugar

½ tsp. salt

Wash petals and leaves carefully under cold running water. Drain thoroughly.

Put drained petals and leaves into salad bowl, cover, and chill. When flowers are thoroughly chilled, combine oil, vinegar, sugar, and salt, and pour over flowers. Toss lightly, and serve immediately.

STUFFED-NASTURTIUM SALAD

1 large bowl	1 Tbs. minced parsley
1 doz. large nasturtium blossoms, prepared for use	½ tsp. black pepper
	Salt (optional)
	2 Tbs. mayonnaise
1 cup canned tuna fish, drained	2 Tbs. olive oil
	1 Tbs. vinegar

½ cup violet leaves, prepared for use

Wash blossoms and leaves carefully under cold running water. Drain thoroughly on paper towels.

In a large bowl, combine tuna fish, parsley, pepper, and mayonnaise.

To fill nasturtiums, hold blossom in palm of hand and use other hand to spoon tuna fish mixture into center of blossom. Press petals down to close blossom, and set on serving platter.

When the blossoms are filled, surround them with violet leaves and sprinkle with oil and vinegar.

Flowers with Meat,
Fish, and Poultry

§ The use of flowers in main dishes may be far older than recorded history—or, at least, recorded culinary history. The ancient Romans, noted for the delight they took in things of the table, happily explored the gustatory possibilities of different kinds of blossoms. One of their recipes calls for the addition of "pounded" rose petals to a whole galaxy of seasonings in what appears to be a calves' brains casserole.

The recipes in this section, however, are of relatively recent origin. From *The Closet of* . . . *Sir Kenelme Digby KT., opened* . . . (*1669*) comes the inspiration for our Marigold Beef Casserole. Sir Kenelme suggests that you "Take good fat Beef, . . . & beat it well with the back of a chopping Knife. Then put it into a pipkin, & cover it with Wine &

Water, & put into it a handfull of good herbs, & an
Onion, & an Anchovie. Let it boil for two hours; a
little before you take it up, put in a few Marygold
flowers; and ſo ſeason it with what ſpice you
please. . . ."

Sir Kenelme and his contemporaries were particularly fond of meat "pyes" and "pasties." Our
Marigold Chicken Pie is adapted from a recipe in
John Nott's *The Cook's and Confectioner's Dictionary* (1723), which directs the cook to parboil
the meat, and then add to it "the Yolks of three
Eggs, Cream, . . . Salt, & Sugar, . . . Flower
Water, & . . . then have a Puff-Paſte ready made,
& roll it into the Form you would have. . . ."

The addition of flower ingredients to fish is especially successful, because the flavor of most kinds
of fish is itself so delicate. Our recipe for Nastur-
tium-Poached Flounder, for example, is adapted
from a recipe in Robert Smith's *Court Cookery*
(1723), which suggests combining the fish and
flowers with "some ſliced Onion & Lemon, some
Parſley, Cives, Bay-Leaf, Baſil, Cloves, Pepper,
. . . two Glaſſes of White wine, a little Vinegar,
and as much Water as will just cover them."

HERBED PORK CHOPS IN ROSE SAUCE

4 large pork chops	1 tsp. parsley flakes
1 Tbs. minced shallots	½ tsp. rosemary
Salt	⅛ cup rose water
Pepper	¼ cup water
	¼ tsp. mace

Trim some of the fat from 4 large pork chops, and heat bits of fat in a heavy skillet. Brown the chops on both sides in this fat. When chops are browned well, remove from pan. Use paper towels to absorb the grease from the chops. Remove fat bits from the pan.

Replace chops in frying pan. Add minced shallots, salt and pepper to taste, mace, parsley, rosemary, rose water, and plain water. Bring to the simmering point. Cover and simmer for 1 hour or until chops are done.

Transfer meat to serving platter. With a wire whisk, scrape up the bits clinging to the pan. Pour rose sauce over meat and serve.

ORANGE-FLOWER DUCK

1 duck (4 to 5 lbs.)
Salt
⅓ cup orange-flower
    butter
3 Tbs. minced onion
4 cups bread crumbs
½ cup chopped celery
1 tsp. grated orange
    rind

½ tsp. sage
1 tsp. salt
½ tsp. black pepper
1 tsp. orange-flower
    water
2 to 3 Tbs. orange juice
3 Tbs. orange-flower
    honey
1 tsp. lemon juice

Preheat oven to 325° F.

Wash duck inside and out, and wipe with damp towel. Rub inside lightly with some salt.

Melt butter in skillet, and sauté onions to a golden brown. Add bread crumbs. Stir quickly for a moment or two, and remove from heat. Put bread-crumb mixture into a large bowl. Add celery, orange rind, sage, salt, pepper, orange-flower water, and mix together thoroughly. Sprinkle with about half the orange juice, and set aside.

When stuffing has cooled, stuff duck carefully and truss. Place on rack in roasting pan, cover with aluminum foil, and bake in oven for 3 hours.

About half an hour before duck is done, warm

honey in a small saucepan, and stir in lemon juice and remaining orange juice. Remove aluminum foil, and brush outside of bird with honey mixture. Return to oven, uncovered, for 30 minutes longer.

MARIGOLD BEEF CASSEROLE

1 flameproof casserole	1 sweet red pepper,
4 short ribs of beef	cut in small squares
3 Tbs. cooking oil	1 tsp. salt
1 large onion,	½ tsp. pepper
cut in rings	1 cup water
1 green pepper,	1 cup white wine
cut in small squares	¾ cup rice

½ tsp. powdered marigold (p. 29)

Preheat oven to 350° F.

Brown short ribs in cooking oil in a flameproof casserole. When meat is nearly brown, add onion rings and cut peppers and cook until onion is transparent. Sprinkle with salt and pepper.

Add water and wine to casserole along with rice and powdered marigold. Stir in well.

Cover and bake 1½ hours or until meat and rice are done.

NASTURTIUM-POACHED
FLOUNDER FILLET

2 lbs. flounder fillets	⅓ cup nasturtium
2 whole cloves	butter
1 bay leaf	3 Tbs. flour
1 cup dry white wine	½ cup cream
1 small onion, minced	1 Tbs. minced parsley
1 tsp. salt	1 Tbs. capers
Dash of black pepper	1 tsp. powdered
Paper towels	nasturtium petals

Wash and clean fish and set on paper towels to drain. When fish has drained, place in shallow pan. Add cloves, bay leaf, wine, onion, salt, and pepper, and just enough water to cover fish. Cover, set over low heat, and let simmer until fish flakes easily under fork.

Meanwhile, melt butter in small saucepan. When butter has melted, gradually stir in flour and cream. Keep stirring until sauce is smooth and very slightly thickened. Add parsley, capers, and powdered petals, stir, and let simmer 2 to 3 minutes.

When fish is done, lift it carefully onto a heated platter. Pour sauce over fish, and serve immediately.

BRAISED BEEF WITH DAYLILIES

1½ lbs. round steak, cut in strips	1 medium onion, sliced
Salt	1 carrot, sliced
Pepper	Parsley sprigs
4 Tbs. butter	1 cup daylily petals
2 cups beef bouillon	1 tsp. arrowroot
	1 Tbs. water

Sprinkle beef strips with salt and pepper. Heat butter in a large frying pan that can be covered tightly. Brown meat strips on both sides in the butter. Pour in beef bouillon. Meat should be covered. Add water if necessary. Simmer gently for 45 minutes, then add the sliced onion, carrot, parsley sprigs and the daylily petals. Continue cooking for 45 additional minutes, or until beef is tender.

When meat is tender, remove beef strips and daylilies to a serving platter. Boil down sauce to 1½ cups and pour through a strainer, mashing the vegetables into the sauce. Skim fat off sauce.

Blend arrowroot and water, and stir into sauce. Cook 2 minutes, stirring constantly. Pour sauce over beef and daylilies, and serve.

STUFFED BREAST OF VEAL
À LA ROSE

4 Tbs. butter
½ cup minced onion
¼ cup raisins
¼ cup pitted and
    diced dates
1½ cups cooked rice
Salt
Pepper
¼ tsp. mace

3 Tbs. minced parsley,
    or 1 Tbs. parsley
    flakes
⅛ cup rose water
    (p. 26)
1 breast of veal, boned
4 slices of bacon,
    blanched
1½ cups chicken broth

Set oven at 300° F.

Heat the butter in a large frying pan. Add the onion and cook until transparent. Add the raisins, and dates and cook 5 minutes longer.

Remove from heat and mix in rice, salt and pepper to taste, mace, and parsley. Add the rose water and stir well. Place this stuffing on one half of the veal breast. Fold over the other half and close with small skewers or by sewing.

Put the meat on a rack in a roasting pan. Place the blanched bacon over the top of the veal, and add the broth. Bake, covered, for 1¾ hours, then remove cover and continue cooking for approximately 30 minutes. Discard bacon before serving veal.

FLOWER-STUFFED SWORDFISH

4 Tbs. rose butter	¼ cup fresh flower
½ cup minced onion	petals (rose or violet)
⅓ cup milk	8 swordfish steaks
½ cup bread crumbs	(about ½ lb. each)
½ tsp. mace	Juice of one lemon
1 tsp. salt	Additional flower petals
1 Tbs. minced parsley	for garnish (optional)

Preheat oven to 375° F.

Melt half the butter in a frying pan, and sauté onion. When onion is golden, add the milk, and stir in the bread crumbs, mace, salt, parsley, and flower petals. Let simmer for 2 to 3 minutes, then set aside.

Arrange four swordfish steaks in a greased baking dish. Spread heaping spoonful of stuffing in the center of each. Cover each steak with another, and skewer together each pair. Dot with remaining butter, and sprinkle with lemon juice. Cover dish with aluminum foil and bake for about 30 minutes, or until fish flakes easily under fork. Baste occasionally.

When fish is done, transfer to heated platter, garnish with additional flower petals (if desired), and serve.

LAMB STEW WITH VIOLET LEAVES AND MARIGOLD BLOSSOMS

4 Tbs. butter

2 lbs. shoulder of lamb, cut in 2-in. pieces for stewing

Salt

Pepper

3 shallots, minced

8 green onions

6 carrots, diced

6 medium potatoes, cut in quarters

2½ cups beef broth

½ cup tender young violet leaves

3 Tbs. marigold blossoms

Flour and water mixed to form a thin paste (optional)

Melt the butter in a Dutch oven.

Sprinkle the chunks of meat with salt and pepper as desired. Brown the lamb pieces on all sides in the heated butter. When the meat is almost browned, add the minced shallots and cook for a minute or two with the lamb.

Pour in beef broth, cover tightly, and simmer 1 hour. Place the lamb and shallots on a separate platter. Cook the green onions and carrots in the Dutch oven for 5 minutes. Add the quartered potatoes and violet leaves, the meat and shallots. Stir carefully to mix. Add marigold blossoms and cook, covered, for 30 minutes.

If a slightly thickened gravy is desired, stir in the thin flour paste just before serving. Serve the stew on heated plates.

VEAL CUTLETS WITH ORANGE-BLOSSOM SAUCE

4 large veal cutlets	½ tsp. powdered thyme
4 Tbs. butter	⅛ cup orange-blossom
Salt	water (p. 26)
Pepper	⅛ cup water
Watercress for garnish (optional)	

Pound cutlets with a mallet or some heavy object.

Melt butter in a large frying pan. When butter is hot, brown cutlets thoroughly on both sides. Continue browning until veal is almost cooked through.

Salt and pepper the meat to taste and sprinkle with thyme.

Add orange-blossom water and the plain water. Bring liquid to the simmering point, cover, and cook gently for 15 minutes.

Place cutlets on a serving platter. With a wire whisk, scrape pan to loosen bits clinging to the bottom. Pour sauce over the meat. Serve garnished with watercress.

ORANGE-BLOSSOM GLAZED
LAMB ROAST

2 shallots, cut in slivers   ¼ cup butter
1 leg of lamb   1 tsp. dried mint leaves
Salt   1 tsp. grated orange
Pepper   peel
          ½ cup orange-blossom preserves

Preheat oven to 450° F.

Insert slivers of shallots in a leg of lamb (half leg may be used). Season with salt and pepper.

Sear the meat on a rack in a roasting pan for 20 minutes. Remove and reset oven for 350° F.

Meanwhile melt the preserves and butter together in a small saucepan. Add the mint leaves and orange peel and cook 5 minutes.

Brush some of the orange-blossom-mint mixture on the meat and replace lamb in oven. Roast for 2 hours or until meat thermometer registers 170°. Baste often during the cooking process with the orange-blossom mixture.

LEMON-HONEY CHICKEN

1 chicken (4 to 5 lbs.)	⅓ cup honey
Salt	1 tsp. lemon juice
¼ cup butter	1 Tbs. rose water
1 lemon	

Preheat oven to 400° F.

Wash chicken thoroughly under cold running water. Wipe with damp paper towel. Rub inside lightly with some salt. Place chicken in pan lined with aluminum foil.

Melt butter in small saucepan, and stir in honey and lemon juice. Remove from heat, and add rose water. Brush outside of chicken with mixture, and place in oven.

After 10 minutes, reduce oven temperature to 325° F. Baste chicken with pan drippings and any leftover honey mixture. Cover pan and return to oven. Allow 40 to 50 minutes per pound. (A roast thermometer will register 180° when chicken is done.)

Before serving, garnish with thin slices of lemon.

VENISON STEW, MARIGOLD

Shoulder of venison	1 cup water
5 Tbs. butter	2 carrots, sliced
Flour	6 mushrooms
Salt	3 sprigs parsley
Pepper	½ tsp. pulverized mari-
2 shallots minced fine	gold
1 cup beef bouillon	8 small white onions

Cut the shoulder into 2-inch cubes, or have the butcher do this job for you.

Heat the butter in a heavy stew pot.

Meanwhile, dredge the venison in a mixture of flour, salt, and pepper, coating each piece thoroughly. Brown the meat cubes on all sides in the hot butter to a rich dark color. Brown the shallots for a minute or two. Pour in the bouillon and water. Simmer gently 2½ hours or until meat is tender. Add vegetables, parsley, and pulverized marigold during the last half hour of cooking.

When venison is tender, remove to serving platter. Boil liquid down to 1 cup and skim off fat. Pour over meat, and serve.

BAKED HALIBUT ROSE

2 lbs. halibut steak	½ cup sliced white
Flour	onions
3 to 4 Tbs. rose butter	2 Tbs. minced parsley
(or plain butter)	1 cup dry rose wine
1 cup sliced mushrooms	½ tsp. salt
1 minced garlic clove	1 tsp. rose water

¼ cup fresh rose petals

Set oven at 300° F.

Wash the fish in cold running water, and drain on paper towels. Dredge fish lightly in flour, place in greased shallow baking pan, and dot with butter on both sides. Bake for 15 minutes.

Remove the baking dish from the oven, and add the mushrooms, garlic, onions, parsley, wine, salt, and rose water. Cover the dish with aluminum foil (or greased brown wrapping paper), and return to oven. Bake for 30 minutes, or until fish flakes easily under fork. Baste often.

When fish is done, lift it carefully onto a serving platter, and spoon the liquid over it. Garnish with fresh rose petals and serve.

MARIGOLD-SCALLOPED
OYSTERS

½ cup marigold butter
1 cup bread crumbs
1 tsp. marigold water
½ cup cracker crumbs
2 Tbs. minced parsley

½ cup finely chopped celery
¼ cup cream
½ tsp. powdered marigold petals

2 cups minced oysters

Preheat oven to 350° F.

Melt butter in small saucepan, and stir in bread crumbs, marigold water, cracker crumbs, and parsley. Remove from heat.

In a shallow greased baking dish, arrange a layer of oysters. Top with thin layer of chopped celery and 1 tablespoon of butter mixture. Repeat process until oysters are used up.

Add cream to remaining butter mixture, and pour over oysters. Sprinkle with powdered petals, cover with aluminum foil, and bake for 20 minutes. Remove foil 5 minutes before taking dish from oven.

VIOLET STUFFED TURKEY

1 turkey (10–12 lbs.)	1 cup bread crumbs
Salt	1 Tbs. fennel seeds
2½ lbs. ground lean	1 tsp. salt
pork	1 tsp. black pepper

2 tsps. violet water

Preheat oven to 325° F.

Wash turkey well, inside and out. Wipe with damp cloth, and rub with some salt, inside and out.

In a large bowl, combine pork, bread crumbs, fennel seeds, salt, pepper, and 1 teaspoon of violet water. Mold into loaf for stuffing. (The addition of a few drops of cold water will help keep it in shape.)

Stuff turkey, and truss carefully. Place turkey inside greased brown-paper bag, and tie end of bag with string. Place in roasting pan, and cook for 3½ to 4 hours (20 minutes per pound). To check doneness, make small slit in top of paper bag. Five minutes before removing turkey from oven, enlarge slit in bag and sprinkle remaining violet water on outside of turkey.

MARIGOLD CHICKEN PIE

2 cups flour

1 tsp. salt

1½ tsps. baking powder

⅔ cups shortening

½ cup lukewarm water

1 egg yolk

2 cups cooked chicken, sliced

1 cup cooked peas

3 Tbs. marigold butter

1 cup mushrooms, sliced

2 Tbs. flour

1 cup milk

1 Tbs. marigold water

½ tsp. salt

Dash of black pepper

1 egg, beaten

½ cup cooked carrots, sliced

Prepare dough for pie shell by sifting together flour, salt, and baking powder into a large bowl. With pastry blender (or two knives), cut in the shortening. Add water, one or two teaspoonfuls at a time, stirring until flour mixture is completely moistened. Add egg yolk, and stir lightly with fork until blended. Press dough into a ball, and chill.

In a large bowl, combine chicken, peas, and carrots. Heat some marigold butter in a skillet, and sauté mushrooms. Drain, and add to chicken and vegetables.

Using same butter in which mushrooms have been sautéed (or adding more if necessary), prepare sauce. When butter is thoroughly dissolved, gradually add flour, stirring until mixture is smooth. Then slowly stir in the milk and marigold water. Season with salt and pepper, and let simmer 2 to 3 minutes longer.

When sauce is done, pour it over the chicken and vegetables, and mix well.

Preheat oven to 350° F.

Take about two-thirds of the dough, and roll out in a circle ⅛-inch thick. Lift dough carefully into two-quart casserole, and pat into place along bottom and sides. (If desired, brush inside of pie shell with beaten egg.) Fill with chicken-vegetable mixture. Roll out remaining dough, again to ⅛-inch thickness. Fold circle lightly in half and carefully place over top of filling. Unfold the dough, and press edges together with edges of bottom shell. With point of sharp knife, cut three or four 1-inch slits in top shell. Brush with beaten egg, and bake for 35 to 40 minutes.

Serve immediately.

Flower Side Dishes

§ John Evelyn was a particularly enthusiastic experimenter with flowers as foods, and many of his results are recorded in his *Acetaria* (1699). His experiments were not always successful, and he observes regretfully, "I once made Macaroons with the ripe blanch'd Seed [of Sunflowers], but the Turpentine did ſo domineer over all that it did not anſwer expectation."

Most of his attempts, however, led to tastier results. Two recipes in this chapter—that for fried heliotrope blossom and that for sunflower buds with lemon-butter sauce—are adaptations of his suggestion that "large Heliotrope and Sun-flower (e're it comes to expand and ſhew its golden Face, . . . is eaten for a dainty . . . fried in freſh Butter criſp with Perſley . . ."

Flower side dishes were popular in the eighteenth

century too, and the recipe for roséed spinach is adapted from one in a manuscript collection of medical and cookery recipes of that period which begins "Boil ʃpinach with white wine until ʃoft. Strain, add Rosewater, Sugar, Cinamon, boil until thick as Marmalad. . . ." And the recipe for brandied blossom fritters is only one version of a dish which has for centuries been regarded as a great delicacy in France and Italy.

ORIENTAL RICE

3 cups water	1 Tbs. rose water
1 tsp. powdered rose	(p. 26)
petals	1 cup pickled daylily
1 tsp. salt	buds (p. 34)

1 cup rice

Place water in pan with close-fitting lid, and bring to boil. When water is at boiling point, stir in powdered petals, rose water, and salt. Add rice, cover, and lower heat to minimum. Let rice simmer, covered, until it is dry and flaky (about 25 minutes, or as package directions recommend).

Add pickled buds to cooked rice, mix together, and serve.

FLOWER RICE RING

2 Tbs. butter	1 tsp. salt
1 cup chopped	¼ tsp. black pepper
mushrooms	2 eggs
1 Tbs. chopped parsley	3 cups cooked rice
¼ cup cream	3 Tbs. shredded fresh
1 cup canned salmon	violet petals,
1 Tbs. violet water	prepared for use
(p. 26)	1 ring mold

Preheat oven to 325°.

Heat butter in skillet, and sauté mushrooms for 2 to 3 minutes. Drain on paper towels.

In a large mixing bowl, combine mushrooms, parsley, cream, salmon, violet water, salt, and pepper. Beat eggs until light and frothy, and add to mixture. Stir lightly until completely blended.

Place one cup of cooked rice in bottom of greased ring mold, and top with layer (about ⅓ of salmon-mushroom mixture. Repeat process until rice and mixture are used up. Set mold in pan containing about 1 inch of water, and place in oven. Bake 1 hour.

Invert onto a platter. Garnish ring with shredded fresh petals, and serve.

MARIGOLD RICE

4 cups chicken broth
  or consommé
4 Tbs. butter
1 minced garlic clove
1 cup uncooked rice

1 tsp. powdered
  marigold petals
2 Tbs. fresh marigold
  petals, prepared for
  use

1 tsp. salt

Put chicken broth in saucepan with close-fitting lid, and bring to just under a boil. Lower heat, and let simmer.

Heat butter in skillet and sauté garlic. When garlic is golden, add rice, stirring constantly until rice too turns golden. Add rice to chicken broth, stir in powdered marigold petals and salt. Cover and let simmer, without stirring, until rice absorbs all the liquid and is dry and flaky (25 to 30 minutes).

Garnish with fresh petals, and serve.

ROSÉED SPINACH

1½ lbs. spinach
1 Tbs. rose butter
  (p. 28)
3 Tbs. rose cooking oil

1 minced garlic clove
¼ cup raisins
1 tsp. salt
Dash of black pepper

Wash spinach well in several waters to remove all traces of sand. Drain, and place in cooking pot. If spinach is young and tender, do not add water. If it is old, cover with boiling water. In either case, cover tightly and cook over medium heat until spinach is barely tender. Drain thoroughly.

Heat butter and oil in a skillet, and sauté garlic. When garlic is golden, add drained spinach and raisins. Season with salt and pepper, and mix together well to assure that spinach is thoroughly coated with butter-oil mixture. Cook over low heat for 3 minutes.

Serve immediately.

ROSE-GLAZED CARROTS

10 small carrots	⅓ cup rose sugar
⅓ cup rose butter	(p. 28)
(p. 28)	2 fresh mint sprigs

Wash carrots well, and scrape thoroughly. Set in saucepan with boiling water to cover. Cook until tender (about 20 minutes). Drain.

Melt butter in saucepan, and gradually stir in sugar. When thoroughly blended, add carrots and let simmer over very low heat until carrots are soft and glazed (about 15 minutes).

Before serving, garnish with mint sprigs.

FLOWER-STUFFED PEPPERS

6 large green peppers
1½ cups canned tuna fish
2 cups cooked rice
2 Tbs. minced fresh carnation petals, prepared for use

3 Tbs. carnation butter (p. 28)
2 small onions, chopped
2 Tbs. flour
1¼ cups milk
½ tsp. dry mustard
1 cup water

2 Tbs. carnation cooking oil (p. 33)

Cut a thin slice from stem end of each pepper. Wash peppers inside and out under cold running water. Remove seeds. Put peppers in saucepan with boiling salted water to cover. Cook over medium heat until barely tender (7 to 8 minutes). Drain.

In a large bowl, combine tuna fish, rice, and minced petals. Sprinkle with about half the carnation oil.

Preheat oven to 350° F.

Heat butter in saucepan, and sauté onion. When onion turns golden, gradually stir in flour. Add milk slowly, stirring constantly until sauce is smooth and thickened. Add mustard and stir.

Pour sauce over tuna-fish mixture, and mix together well. Fill each pepper loosely (do not press in stuffing), and set each upright in a shallow baking dish. Sprinkle remaining carnation oil and about ¼ cup of water over peppers. Pour rest of water into bottom of dish.

Bake for 25 minutes, and serve.

GOLDEN-FRIED VIOLETS

2 lemons	3 seedless oranges
3 cups violet leaves and petals, prepared for use	3 Tbs. butter
	½ tsp. salt
	1 Tbs. sugar

2 sprigs fresh mint

Peel the lemons and oranges and trim off the white membrane. Cut into thin slices and, with the point of a knife, remove the pits from the lemon slices.

Wash violet leaves and petals in cold running water, and drain on paper towels.

Melt butter in a large frying pan, and sauté the fruit slices for 2 to 3 minutes. Add violet leaves and petals, salt, and sugar, and fry for 3 to 4 minutes more.

Before serving, garnish with fresh mint sprigs.

BRANDIED BLOSSOM
FRITTERS

3 cups fresh blossoms (elder, rose, violet, or squash), prepared for use	1 cup flour
	1 tsp. salt
	2 egg yolks
	2 Tbs. cooking oil
2 oz. fruit brandy	½ cup beer
2 Tbs. sugar	Water
½ tsp. cinnamon	3 egg whites

6 Tbs. cooking oil

Wash blossoms under cold running water, and drain. Spread blossoms on large platter, and sprinkle with brandy, sugar, and cinnamon.

Sift flour and salt into large bowl. Beat egg yolks lightly, and add oil. Stir egg mixture into flour. Add beer gradually, and stir until batter is smooth. Add a few drops of lukewarm water, to keep batter thin. Beat egg whites until they peak, and fold them into the batter.

Heat oil in a skillet. Dip the blossoms into the batter, one at a time, and sauté. Drain, and arrange on serving platter.

BROCCOLI WITH LEMON-FLOWER SAUCE

1 bunch broccoli (about 1½ lbs.)	½ tsp. salt
	Dash of black pepper
3 Tbs. lemon-flower butter (p. 28)	2 Tbs. shredded lemon-flower petals,
2 Tbs. flour	prepared for use

1 cup milk

Wash broccoli in cold running water, and drain. Trim off large leaves and tough ends of stalks. Place stalks upright in deep saucepan, and add 2 inches of salted water. Cover, and cook over medium heat until stalks can be pierced with a fork (about 20 minutes). Remove from heat, and drain.

Melt butter in small saucepan over low heat. Gradually stir in flour, and keep stirring until mixture is smooth. Add milk gradually, stirring constantly until sauce begins to thicken. Add salt and pepper, and let simmer for 3 to 4 minutes longer.

Pour sauce over cooked broccoli. Before serving, garnish with shredded fresh petals.

ORANGE-FLOWER BEETS

1 saucepan
½ cup orange juice
2 Tbs. orange-flower
   butter
¼ cup sugar
2 Tbs. flour

1 tsp. orange-flower
   water
3 cups sliced beets
1 Tbs. shredded fresh
   orange-flower petals
   (optional)

Preheat oven to 350° F.

Warm orange juice in small saucepan over low heat, and stir in butter. When butter is completely melted, gradually add sugar and flour, stirring constantly until blended. Add orange-flower water, and stir.

Set beets in baking dish, and add orange-flower mixture. Cover dish with aluminum foil and bake for 15 minutes.

Before serving, garnish with shredded orange-flower petals.

CHRYSANTHEMUMS NIPPONESE

1 dozen yellow
   chrysanthemums,
   prepared for use

1 tsp. salt
½ tsp. orange-flower
   water

Soy sauce

Remove stems and discard; retain leaves. Wash the blossoms and leaves with cold running water, and drain.

Place about 1 inch of salted water in saucepan with tightly fitting lid. Bring water to boil, and add blossoms and leaves. Cover, and let simmer over low heat until flowers are tender (about 12 minutes).

Drain blossoms, and sprinkle with orange-flower water and soy sauce. Serve on steamed rice, with additional soy sauce.

SUNFLOWER BUDS WITH LEMON-BUTTER SAUCE

4 cups fresh sunflower
   buds, prepared for use
¼ cup butter
3 Tbs. lemon juice
½ tsp. salt
¼ tsp. black pepper
2 Tbs. minced fresh
   mint leaves

Wash buds in cold running water, and drain.

Place about 1 inch of salted water in saucepan with close-fitting lid. Bring water to a boil, and add sunflower buds. Cover, and let simmer until buds are easily pierced with fork. Drain, and put buds on serving dish.

Melt butter in small saucepan. Add lemon juice, salt, pepper, and mint, and stir. Pour sauce over buds and serve.

FRIED DANDELION LEAVES

1 lb. dandelion leaves	1 tsp. salt
3 Tbs. salad oil	½ tsp. black pepper
1 green onion, chopped	2 Tbs. grated
1 garlic clove, minced	Parmesan cheese

Cut dandelion leaves into 3-inch pieces. Wash in cold running water, and drain.

Put about 1 inch of water into saucepan, add ¾ tsp. salt, and bring to a boil. Add dandelion leaves, lower heat, and let simmer until leaves are tender (about 12 minutes). Drain, and set aside.

Heat oil in large skillet, and sauté onion and garlic. When onion is golden, add dandelion leaves, remaining salt, and pepper, and cook over medium flame for 5 minutes, stirring occasionally.

Serve with grated cheese.

MARIGOLD CARROTS WITH ALMONDS

1 can condensed milk (14 oz.) and equal quantity of water	3 Tbs. chopped blanched almonds
2 cups grated raw carrots	1 tsp. salt
	½ tsp. powdered marigold petals
1 cup marigold butter	1 Tbs. lemon juice

Combine condensed milk and equal quantity of water in saucepan. Set over low heat, and bring to just under a boil. Add grated carrots, lower heat, and let simmer for 40 minutes, stirring often.

When carrots are tender, gradually add butter, stirring constantly. When butter is completely melted, stir in almonds and salt.

Dissolve powdered marigold in lemon juice, and add to carrot mixture. Let simmer 5 minutes more.

Serve hot.

FRIED HELIOTROPE BLOSSOMS

4 cups fresh heliotrope blossoms, prepared for use	2 Tbs. chopped parsley
	1 tsp. salt
	½ tsp. black pepper
3 Tbs. butter	1 tsp. heliotrope water
1 Tbs. lemon juice	

Wash heliotrope blossoms in cold running water, and drain.

Melt butter in skillet, and gently ease in the blossoms (one or two at a time so as not to crush them). Sprinkle the lemon juice, parsley, salt, and pepper over the blossoms, and cook over low heat until blossoms are tender (about 10 minutes). Drain cooked blossoms on paper towels.

Arrange blossoms on serving platter, and sprinkle with heliotrope water. Serve immediately.

MARIGOLD POTATO PUFF

6 large potatoes	1 tsp. salt
1 bay leaf	½ tsp. black pepper
1¼ cups milk	2 eggs
4 Tbs. butter	1 Tbs. shredded fresh
1 tsp. powdered	marigold petals,
marigold petals	prepared for use
(p. 29)	1 Casserole

Peel potatoes, cut in quarters, and cover with boiling salted water. Add bay leaf, and cook until tender. Then drain potatoes, discard bay leaf, and mash potatoes thoroughly. Be sure no lumps remain.

Preheat oven to 350° F.

Heat milk in small saucepan. Dissolve butter and powdered petals in heated milk, and stir mixture into mashed potatoes. Add salt and pepper.

Separate eggs, and beat yolks until thick and lemon-colored. Beat yolks into mashed potatoes. Now beat egg whites until they peak; fold into mashed potatoes.

Bake, in greased casserole, until puffed and golden brown (about 30 minutes). Before serving, sprinkle with shredded fresh petals.

AMERICAN COWSLIP* LEAVES WITH CREAM SAUCE

3 cups American cowslip leaves, prepared for use	1 cup milk or light cream
2 Tbs. butter	1 Tbs. minced parsley
2 Tbs. flour	½ tsp. dry mustard
	1 tsp. salt

½ tsp. black pepper

Wash leaves in cold running water, and drain. Place in saucepan, cover with boiling salted water (approximately ¼ tsp. salt to 1 cup water), and bring to a boil again. Drain, and repeat process twice more, using fresh unsalted water each time.

Melt butter in small saucepan, and stir in flour. Gradually add milk, stirring constantly until completely blended and smooth. Add parsley, mustard, salt, and pepper, and stir until slightly thickened.

Remove sauce from heat, pour over drained leaves, and serve.

* The American Cowslip is known as marsh marigold.

PEAS WITH WATER-LILY BUDS

1 cup water-lily buds, prepared for use	Salt
	2 Tbs. cooking oil
2 cups peas	1 Tbs. chopped parsley

Wash buds in cold running water, and drain on paper towels.

Put buds in saucepan, and cover with boiling salted water (approximately ¼ tsp. salt to 1 cup of water). Bring to a boil again, and drain. Repeat process twice more, using fresh unsalted water each time.

Put peas in saucepan with about 1 inch boiling water. Cover, and cook over low heat until barely tender. Drain.

Heat oil in skillet, and add drained peas and buds. Shake skillet gently to mix (a utensil may damage the peas or buds). Add parsley and ½ teaspoon salt, and cook 3 to 4 minutes.

LEMON-ORANGE VIOLETS

3 cups fresh violet leaves and petals, prepared for use	3 Tbs. butter
	½ tsp. salt
	1 Tbs. sugar
1 large lemon	1 Tbs. minced mint
2 oranges	leaves

Wash violet leaves and petals in cold running water, and drain. Peel lemon and oranges, slice thin, and with a sharp knife remove pits and trim off white membrane.

Melt butter in skillet, sauté fruit slices, and drain. Add violet leaves and petals, salt and sugar, and cook over low heat until flowers are tender (about 10 minutes). Add fruit slices and minced mint and cook for 3 minutes more. Serve immediately.

DAYLILIES ORIENTAL STYLE

2 cups fresh daylily   ½ cup slivered water
  buds, prepared for use   chestnuts
3 Tbs. butter   ½ tsp. salt
       ½ tsp. black pepper

Wash buds in cold running water, and drain on paper towels.

Put buds in saucepan and add boiling salted water to cover (approximately ¼ tsp. salt to 1 cup of water). Bring to a boil again, reduce heat, and cook for 5 minutes longer. Drain.

Melt butter in skillet, and add water chestnuts. Cook over low heat for 7 to 8 minutes. Add buds, and mix well until buds are thoroughly covered with butter. Cook a minute or two longer.

Before serving, season with salt and pepper.

Flower Breads, Cookies, Cakes, Pies, and Other Delights

§ Perhaps the most traditional recipe in this chapter is the one for Apple-Rose Pie. Pies, or tarts, as they were called in the sixteenth and seventeenth centuries, were easily the favorite dessert of the hearty eaters of early England. Husbands who today demand "apple pie like the one Grandma used to make" are merely carrying on in grand style as men did three hundred years ago.

Then, as now, there was scarcely a man who didn't favor apple pie—always seasoned in early days with rose water—high above other pies. Gervase Markham in his famous cookery book, *The English Hus-wife*, originally published in 1615, cited recipes for both Green Apple Tart and Pippin Tart. ("Pippin," a word uncommon now, was a name used for numerous varieties of apple.)

An anonymous cookbook author, contemporary

119

with Markham, gave the apple-tart recipe that was the inspiration for our Apple-Rose Pie. Here is the gist of it:

> Pare apples, slice. Boil until thick with white wine, sugar, cinnamon, rose water. Cook and strain. Beat well. Put in tart shell.

For readers who would like to compare our anonymous author's approach with Markham's, here is the Pippin Tart from *The English Hus-wife*:

> Pare, core and halve pippins. Lay face down in tart ſhell and dot with cloveſ, cinnamon bits and butter. Cover with ſuger and preſs dough edges together. Bake. Boil butter and roſe water together and bruſh on tart, ſprinkle on sugar. Bake and ſerve.

APPLE-ROSE PIE

6 large apples	2 eggs, separated
⅓ cup granulated sugar	Baked 8-inch pie shell
1 Tbs. white wine	1 Tbs. water
1½ tsps. rose water	4 Tbs. sugar
(p. 26)	Pinch of salt
¼ tsp. mace	¼ tsp. cream of tartar
3 Tbs. butter	1 fine sieve

Crystallized rose petals (p. 144)

Preheat oven to 375° F.

Peel, core, and slice the apples, then place them in a saucepan with ⅓ cup sugar, the wine, rose water, and mace. Simmer gently until apples are tender, then strain through a fine sieve.

Return strained apple mixture to saucepan and reheat. Next, stir in the butter and egg yolks. Cook until the mixture thickens.

Pour apple filling into the prepared pie shell and bake about 20 to 25 minutes or until filling is set.

Meanwhile, beat the egg whites with 1 Tbs. water and a pinch of salt until foam appears. Add cream of tartar and beat until stiff peaks form. Gradually beat in 4 Tbs. sugar. Keep beating until meringue holds its shape.

Spoon meringue over pie and decorate with crystallized rose petals. Replace pie in oven and bake until meringue is lightly browned.

ROSE-GERANIUM CAKE

Fresh rose-geranium
    leaves
2 cups cake flour
3 tsps. baking powder
¼ tsp. salt
2½ Tbs. hydrogenated
    shortening
1 cup sugar
1 egg, plus 2 egg yolks
    (at room tempera-
    ture)
2 tsps. rose water
    (p. 26)

3 drops almond extract
1 cup milk (at
    room temperature)
Rose preserves

¼ cup rose-geranium
    butter (see recipe
    below)
2 cups sifted
    confectioner's sugar
2 drops almond extract
Cream (approximately
    2 tsps.)

Red food coloring

Set oven at 350° F.

Grease two 9-inch layer-cake pans, and dust lightly with flour. Place 2 geranium leaves in each pan.

Sift cake flour with baking powder and salt into a bowl. Set the sifter and the bowl with dry ingredients aside.

Cream shortening with sugar, and beat until the mixture is very light and fluffy. Then add the whole egg and the egg yolks one at a time, beating well after each addition. When the eggs and batter have been thoroughly blended, add the rose water and almond extract.

Now sift the dry ingredients into the batter, adding them alternately with the milk. Stir gently to mix thoroughly, but be careful not to overbeat. Pour the batter into the prepared cake pans and bake 20 to 25 minutes, or until cake tests done.

Cool cake layers in pans 10 minutes; then remove to cooling racks. When the layers are thoroughly cooled, put them together with rose preserves.

Frosting:

To prepare the geranium frosting, cream softened geranium butter in a small electric mixer bowl. Combine butter and sugar at low speed. Add almond extract, and beat at high speed until the frosting is very light, adding a few drops of cream from time to time. When frosting is light and smooth, tint it a delicate pink with 2 or 3 drops of red coloring.

Rose-Geranium Butter:

Enclose desired amount of sweet butter in fresh, washed rose-geranium leaves. Wrap in a damp cloth and let stand overnight. Unwrap, and butter is ready to use.

SUNFLOWER-SEED COOKIES

½ cup butter, softened
¼ cup granulated sugar
¼ cup light brown
  sugar
1 egg, slightly beaten

1⅓ cups sifted flour
¼ tsp. soda
½ tsp. salt
¾ tsp. vanilla
¼ cup sunflower seeds

Cream the butter, sugar, and beaten egg.

Sift flour, soda and salt. Add sifted ingredients to creamed mixture. Add vanilla and stir in. Mix sunflower seeds into the dough, stirring carefully. If necessary, mix with hands.

Form the dough into a roll approximately 2 inches in diameter. Enclose roll in waxed paper. Chill overnight, or at least 5 hours.

When roll is well chilled, preheat oven to 400° F. Cut cookies in slices ⅛ inch thick. Use an ungreased cookie sheet and set cookies slightly apart. Bake about 7 minutes until cookies are browned.

ROSE WAFERS

½ cup butter, softened
½ cup sugar
1 egg
¾ cup flour

Pinch of salt
1 Tbs. rose water
  (p. 26)
⅛ tsp. allspice

Preheat oven to 375° F.

Cream butter and sugar thoroughly. Beat the egg well with a fork and add to the butter and sugar. Blend in the flour, salt, rose water and allspice.

Place rounded teaspoonfuls of cookie dough on a buttered cookie sheet.

Bake 10 to 15 minutes. Recipe makes approximately 2½ dozen wafers.

ROSE DELIGHT

1 cup rose petals, washed and dried
½ cup cooking oil

Confectioner's sugar
2 sponge-cake layers
Rose preserves

Using a small saucepan, fry a few rose petals at a time in the heated cooking oil. Use tongs to lift them in and out carefully. As soon as the petals are done (about 5 minutes), dip them in confectioner's sugar. Make sure that each petal is entirely coated with the sugar. Continue in this manner until all the rose petals are prepared.

Next, spread one sponge-cake layer thinly with the rose preserves. Place the second layer on top of it. Put a thin coating of preserves on the cake and decorate with the coated rose petals.

LIME-GERANIUM MUFFINS

½ cup tender lime-
   geranium leaves,
   washed and dried
Grated peel of 1 orange
¾ cup warmed water
1 pkg. yeast

⅓ cup sugar
1 tsp. salt
2¼ cups sifted flour
1 egg
¼ cup butter, softened
18 sugar cubes

Melted butter

Chop the geranium leaves with the grated peel in a chopping bowl. Set aside.

Pour warmed water into a large mixing bowl. Stir in the yeast until dissolved.

Add the sugar, salt, and 1 cup of the flour. Beat several minutes. The mixture should fall off the mixing spoon in sheets.

Beat in the egg and softened butter and the rest of the flour.

Butter 18 medium-size muffin cups.

Spoon the batter into each muffin cup, filling about one half full. Make a dent in the top of each muffin.

Roll one of the sugar cubes in the geranium-leaf and orange-peel mixture and place it in one muffin where you made a dent. Continue in this fashion until all of the muffins have been prepared. Brush melted butter over the tops.

Cover and let the dough rise in a warm place until it has doubled in size. This will take about 30 minutes.

Meanwhile, preheat the oven to 375° F. When dough is ready, bake approximately 20 minutes or until muffins are brown.

ORANGE-BLOSSOM-MARIGOLD BREAD

1 loaf pan
4 fresh marigold petals, washed and dried
3 cups sifted flour
½ cup sugar
4 tsps. baking powder
1¼ tsps. salt

½ cup orange-blossom preserves (p. 158)
⅓ cup chopped dates
1 cup milk
2 Tbs. melted butter
1 large egg, slightly beaten

Set oven at 350° F.

Butter a loaf pan and place marigold petals in the bottom, side by side.

Sift flour with the sugar, baking powder and salt. Combine sifted ingredients with the orange-blossom preserves and the chopped dates.

Mix milk, melted butter and beaten egg. Add to orange-blossom mixture. Stir until thoroughly blended, then transfer to the loaf pan and bake 1 hour or until done.

VIOLET CUPCAKES

1 cup sugar

3 egg yolks

1 egg white

2½ Tbs. hydrogenated
    shortening

1½ tsps. violet water
    (p. 26)

1 cup milk

2 cups flour

2½ tsps. baking powder

¼ tsp. salt

White creamy frosting

Crystallized violets
    (p. 144)

Preheat oven to 350° F.

Beat sugar, egg yolk and white, shortening, and violet water thoroughly. Add milk, blending in well.

Sift together the flour, baking powder, and salt. Beat sifted ingredients into the violet mixture.

Pour batter into greased and floured cupcake pan, filling each cup about ⅔ full.

Bake for 20 minutes or until cupcakes spring back when pressed lightly. When cool, frost the cupcakes with white frosting and decorate with crystallized violets.

HEATHER-HONEY BOWS

4 cups flour	1 qt. vegetable oil
Pinch of salt	1 qt. heather honey
¼ lb. butter	(p. 34)
1 egg	Confectioner's sugar

Sift the flour and salt onto a clean surface. Cream the butter and add it and the egg to the flour. Mix thoroughly, adding a few drops of warm water to form dough.

Knead well, then shape the dough into a ball and slice in 4 pieces. Roll out the 4 portions into rectangles ¼ inch thick. Cut into strips lengthwise, and tie each strip into a bow knot.

Fry in smoking hot oil until browned. Lift bows from fat and place on paper towels to cool.

Meanwhile, melt honey in a deep pan, and drop in a few bows. Drain, and remove them to a serving platter. Continue in this manner with all the rest. When the bows are cool, sprinkle confectioner's sugar over them and serve.

Flower Desserts

§ Flower petals and leaves, flower jellies, candied flowers, flower syrups and waters all find their way into these recipes for desserts. If we were to single out the most interesting use of flowers in desserts, however, it would be the way our predecessors used the flower waters in so many different recipes. The use of rose and orange-blossom water dates back to pre-Renaissance days, and was almost a rigid tradition in early cookery. Apparently no cream, custard, flummery, fromage, "white pot," or sillabub was satisfying to the careful taste of the early cook unless it was seasoned with one of these flower waters. Indeed, rose and orange-blossom flavorings were used in the sixteenth, seventeenth, and eighteenth centuries as often as vanilla extract is employed today.

Robert Smith, in writing the recipe for his "Whipt Sillabub, Very Good" (*Court Cookery*, 1723), combined orange-flower water with the juice of a lemon to flavor a froth of cream, sugar, and eggs that was meant to top glasses half filled with Rhenish wine, claret, and sugar.

In *The London Cook* (1762), William Gelleroy presented a Vermicelli Pudding with an assortment of flavorings—mace, lemon rind and, of course, flower water—to heighten the taste of a custard featuring five ounces of vermicelli.

Gelleroy had a wonderful Quaking Pudding that called for a pint of thick cream to be beaten with 10 egg yolks, 3 whites, and rose water. The recipe proceeded from there, evolving into what we hope was a non-quaking custard. A rose-water sauce completed the dish.

John Farley in *The London Art of Cookery* (1783) has a recipe that would awe nearly any contemporary cook. He starts out, "Take a peck of cowslips," then goes on to fashion a cowslip pudding with Naples biscuits, 3 pints of cream, 16 eggs, and rose water.

Rose or orange-flower water could be used in Elizabeth Wilson's gooseberry pudding (1824). Her recipe called for 6 spoons of gooseberry pulp, eggs, sugar, clarified butter, lemon peel, bread crumbs, and the flower water.

VIOLET SNOW

½ cup cold water   1 cup violet syrup
1 envelope gelatin   (p. 32)
    (unflavored)   Salt
            Whites of 2 large eggs

Pour cold water into the top of a double boiler. Soften gelatin by sprinkling it over the water. Heat over boiling water, stirring only until gelatin is dissolved.

Add violet syrup and ¼ tsp. salt to the gelatin mixture, stirring until salt is thoroughly dissolved.

Place ice cubes and water in the bottom part of the double boiler up to the halfway mark. Sprinkle 2½ Tbs. salt over the ice water and replace top section of the double boiler containing the violet mixture. Set aside until mixture resembles unbeaten egg white in consistency.

At this point, add egg whites. Beat well. Mixture should hold its shape.

Spoon into sherbet dishes and chill. You may serve it with a yellow custard sauce flavored with a few drops of violet water if desired.

For Rose Snow: Substitute rose syrup for the violet syrup. Flavor custard sauce with a few drops of rose water.

ROSE FRUIT COMPOTE

6 fresh rose petals,
  washed well
½ cup sliced bananas
½ cup sliced peaches
3 Tbs. lemon juice
½ cup sliced
  strawberries
½ cup cubed pineapple

½ cup blueberries,
  picked over, washed
  and drained
½ cup seedless grapes
1 qt. Rose Snow
  (p. 133)
¼ cup candied roses
  (p. 144)

Place each fresh rose petal in the bottom of a sherbet glass.

In a medium-size bowl, sprinkle banana and peach slices with lemon juice to avoid discoloration. Stir to coat slices evenly with the lemon juice.

Add the remaining fruits and mix well but without crushing the fruit. Spoon into sherbet glasses.

Top each with a small scoop of rose sherbet and garnish with the candied roses, if desired.

GERANIUM CUSTARD

6 small rose-geranium
  leaves

4 eggs
¼ cup sugar

2 cups milk

Preheat oven to 350° F.

Butter 6 custard cups. Place a geranium leaf in the bottom of each cup.

Beat the eggs lightly.

Add the sugar and milk to the eggs. Stir until the sugar is dissolved. Pour into the custard cups over the leaves.

Place the cups in a baking pan. Pour water heated to the simmering point around the cups to the level of the pudding.

Bake 50 minutes or until custard tests done (when a knife placed in the center comes out clean). Cool.

VIOLET DESSERT

4 egg yolks	2 tsps. violet liqueur
¾ cup sugar	6 egg whites

¼ cup crushed candied violets (p. 144)

Preheat oven to 300° F.

Whip the egg yolks together with the sugar until the mixture is pale yellow and thickened.

Add the violet liqueur.

Beat the egg whites until stiff. Fold whites into the violet mixture.

Select an attractive ovenproof platter. Spoon the mixture onto the platter. Smooth mound with a spatula.

Bake for approximately 10 minutes. Sprinkle half the crushed candied violets over the top, evenly or in a pattern. Make a ½-inch-deep slit along the high center portion, spread out, and sprinkle with remaining violets.

Reset oven for 350° F. and replace in oven for 5 minutes. Do not overcook.

ROSE CRÊPES

1 cup flour	1 cup milk
⅓ cup confectioner's sugar	2 eggs
	Rose-petal jelly
¼ tsp. salt	(p. 157)

Sift flour with confectioner's sugar and salt into medium-size mixing bowl. Add milk and stir well. Crêpe batter should be smooth.

Break eggs into mixture and beat very well.

Meanwhile, heat small frying pan. Grease lightly with butter.

Spoon a little of the batter to cover bottom of pan. When crêpe is lightly browned on one side, take a spatula and turn crêpe carefully. Cook on the other side. Remove to dish and keep warm. Continue cooking crêpes one by one.

Spread each crêpe with a thin layer of rose-petal jelly and roll up. Sprinkle with additional confectioner's sugar. Serve from a heated tray.

MARIGOLD RICE PUDDING

4 cups milk
½ cup uncooked rice
3 Tbs. cornstarch
Water

½ cup sugar
6 tiny fresh marigold
  petals, well washed
6 custard cups

Pour milk into medium-size saucepan. Set over low to moderate heat until film forms, approximately 10 minutes, then add rice. Stir slowly until milk reaches the boiling point. Turn heat to very low and cook for 25 minutes.

Combine cornstarch and a little water until a paste is formed. Blend paste into rice mixture. Add sugar. Cook, stirring gently, until custard starts to thicken.

Cool. Meanwhile, place one marigold petal in each of 6 custard cups. Pour rice custard into marigold cups.

ORANGE-CHESTNUT PUDDING

2 cups heavy cream
½ cup confectioner's
  sugar

1 tsp. orange-flower
  water (p. 26)
2 egg whites

⅓ cup crushed canned chestnuts

Whip the cream. It should be well beaten, but not to the point of stiffness.

Mix in the confectioner's sugar and add the orange-flower water.

Beat the egg whites until stiff. Fold egg whites into cream mixture. Add chestnuts.

Place pudding in refrigerator and freeze until firm.

ROSE DESSERT

Fresh rose petals, washed
5 ripe bananas, mashed
1¼ cups chopped dates
1½ cups rose-petal
  preserves

2 Tbs. lemon juice
1 pt. hard-packed
  vanilla ice cream
Candied rose petals
  (p. 144

Use fresh rose petals to line a medium-size cut-crystal bowl.

Mix bananas with chopped dates. Pack this mixture in crystal bowl. Spoon the rose preserves over the top. Sprinkle with lemon juice.

Just before serving, top with small mounds of vanilla ice cream and garnish with candied rose petals.

WHITE ROSE PUDDING

4 cups milk	½ cup powdered sugar
½ cup cornstarch	3 tsps. rose water
1 fine sieve	(p. 26)

Crushed pistachio nuts for garnish (optional)

Pour 3 cups of milk into a saucepan and bring to a temperature just below the boiling point.

Dissolve the starch and sugar in the fourth cup of milk. Blend carefully until well mixed. Spoon in the rose water, then pour through a fine sieve into the heated milk.

Bring mixture to a boil, then simmer 5 minutes, stirring constantly with wooden spoon. Pour into pudding dishes. Sprinkle crushed pistachio nuts over the pudding if desired.

SWEET WAFFLES WITH ROSE-HIP SYRUP

2½ cups sifted flour	2 cups cream
2 tsps. baking powder	4 egg yolks, well beaten
6 Tbs. granulated sugar	¼ cup melted butter
¼ tsp. salt	4 egg whites

3 cups rose-hip syrup (p. 32)

Preheat waffle iron.

Sift together the flour, baking powder, sugar, and salt. Then pour in cream and add egg yolks. Beat well, then add melted butter.

Whip egg whites until stiff. Carefully fold egg whites into cream mixture.

Pour batter from a pitcher or cup onto the center of the hot waffle iron. Bake until done—that is, until steaming has stopped.

Serve with rose-hip syrup.

Flower Confections

§ Today's housewife usually relies on ordinary colored sugars to enhance her desserts. The cook of yesteryear spurned the illusory: she used real blossoms, crystallized, to grace her cookies, tea cakes, tarts, and other pastries. Also, candied petals were treasured as after-dinner treats. Before and after dinner, eager little fingers probably found their way into those tempting jars on the pantry shelves. Candied roses, candied orange blossoms and candied violets may well have been the lollipops of the seventeenth century.

There were two methods of preparing candied flowers. One called for dropping the blossoms into a hot syrup. The other method was somewhat more complicated. It required the cook to dip the flowers into gum arabic or gum dragon, then brush the petals with sugar. Here are examples of each method.

The first, from E. Smith's *Compleat Housewife* (1727) :

"To candy Orange-Flowers :—Take half a pound of double-refin'd ſugar finely beaten, wet it with orange-flower-water, then boil it candy high, then put in a handful of orange-flowers, keeping it ſtirring, but let it not boil, and when the ſugar candies about them, take it off the fire, then drop it on a plate, and set it by till 'tis cold."

Here is Hannah Woolley's version of the gum-arabic method, from *The Accomplis'd Ladies delight* . . . (1675) :

"Take Gum Arabick & ſteep it in Rose-Water all night, the next day take what Flowers or Herbs you pleaſe & dip them well in that Gum water & ſwing them well from it, then ſtrew them very thick with Sugar beaten fine on every ſide, & lay them upon plates to dry in the ſun, & when you find they begin to dry turn them on clean plates, & if you find Sugar wanting ſupply it."

CRYSTALLIZED FLOWER PETALS

Egg white

Granulated sugar

Fresh petals, washed well and dried

Beat egg white well. Brush the egg white onto both sides of the fresh petals. Dip petals in granulated sugar, using tongs and handling carefully. Place petals on a platter and let dry completely in a warm place.

Crystallized flower petals should be stored in airtight containers, preferably with waxed paper between each layer. Use for decorating pastries and other desserts.

ROSE ALMOND PUFFS

1 cup granulated sugar	2 Tbs. butter
1 Tbs. molasses	½ tsp. essence of roses
¼ cup light cream	(p. 30)
¼ cup milk	1 cup roasted
2 Tbs. light corn syrup	unblanched almonds

4 cups puffed rice cereal

Mix sugar, molasses, cream, milk, corn syrup, and butter in a saucepan.

Cook until mixture reaches a temperature of 280° F. on candy thermometer, then remove from the heat. Add essence of roses along with cereal and almonds, and stir well.

With a spatula, spread mixture in an 8-inch square greased baking pan. Cool, then cut in squares.

VIOLET WAFERS

4 Tbs. cold water	½ tsp. essence of violets
1 tsp. unflavored gelatin	(p. 30)
3 tsps. boiling water	Cookie cutters
	Confectioner's sugar

Sprinkle cold water over gelatin and let stand 5 minutes. Add boiling water to dissolve the gelatin. Add essence of violets.

Slowly add confectioner's sugar, enough so that mixture can be kneaded. Knead well, then roll out in a thin sheet on a board that has been well coated with sugar.

Cut in round or fancy shapes. Allow to stand until wafers are brittle and dry.

ORANGE-BLOSSOM FUDGE

2 cups sugar	¼ cup orange-blossom
⅔ cup light corn syrup	water (p. 26)
¼ tsp. salt	2 egg whites
¼ cup water	Waxed paper
	1 cup walnut meats, chopped

Cook the first 4 ingredients over low heat, stirring until sugar is dissolved. Continue to cook, but without stirring, until candy thermometer reaches 265°F. Then add orange-blossom water.

Meanwhile, beat egg whites until stiff.

Blend hot syrup and egg whites by pouring syrup in a steady stream, beating all the while. Continue beating with a wooden spoon until candy holds its shape when dropped from the spoon.

Add chopped nut meats and drop from a teaspoon onto waxed paper.

MARZIPAN HEARTS

Confectioner's sugar	2 tsps. rose water
1 cup almond paste	(p. 26)
1 egg white	Red sugar for baking

Mix first 4 ingredients well, using 2⅔ cups confectioner's sugar. Knead with hands if necessary.

Roll out marzipan on counter or cutting board, as you would roll out dough for cookies. Then cut into heart shapes (or any other desired shape).

Mix red sugar with an equal amount of confectioner's sugar, and dip hearts in this mixture.

Flower Sauces

§ The recipes in this section have been adapted from various sources to suit contemporary American tastes.

The Flower Water Glaze, for example, is very popular in Middle Eastern and Far Eastern cooking. After the poultry is glazed and cooked, you may want to try the Far Eastern method of cutting it into thin slices and dipping each slice into soy sauce at table.

From John Evelyn's *Acetaria* (1699) came the simplest recipe for flower sauce—"a little Rofe-water, less Vinegar, with Butter beaten together, & . . . sweetened with the Sugar caftor." A later author recommends adding "a Jill of Cream, & Lemon peel shred . . ." These form the bases for two of the sauces in this chapter.

149

ROSE CHOCOLATE SAUCE

½ cup water	1 cup sugar
3 oz. unsweetened chocolate	¼ tsp. salt
	1 Tbs. butter

1 tsp. rose water

Put water in saucepan and bring to a boil. Reduce heat and add chocolate, stirring constantly until it melts. Add sugar and salt, and stir until completely dissolved. Boil gently for 5 minutes. Add butter and rose water, and remove from heat.

Serve hot with ice cream.

ORANGE-FLOWER SAUCE

½ cup butter	½ cup orange juice
1 egg	½ cup milk
1½ tsps. grated orange rind	1 tsp. orange-flower water
½ tsp. powdered orange-flower petals	¾ cup sugar
	1 double boiler

Allow butter to stand at room temperature for 10 to 15 minutes.

Beat egg until light and frothy. Add orange rind, powdered petals, orange juice, milk, and orange-flower water, and beat together 1 minute longer.

Cream together butter and sugar. Stir in egg mixture, and keep stirring until completely blended.

Half fill bottom half of double boiler with water, and bring to a boil. Reduce heat. Pour sauce into top half of double boiler, and cook over low heat for 15 minutes.

Let sauce cool to room temperature, and serve over ice cream or sherbet.

FLOWER-WATER GLAZE FOR POULTRY AND HAM

¼ cup butter   ⅓ cup honey
1 Tbs. rose or orange-flower water

Melt butter in a small saucepan, and stir in honey and flower water. Brush lightly over poultry or ham before setting it in the oven.

MARIGOLD CHEESE SAUCE

2 Tbs. butter	1 tsp. powdered
2 Tbs. flour	marigold petals
1¼ cups milk	1¼ cups grated Cheddar
½ tsp. salt	cheese
¼ tsp. black pepper	Rice or noodles

Melt butter in saucepan. Stir in flour, and keep stirring until completely blended. Add milk gradually, stirring constantly, and bring to a boil. Then stir in salt, pepper, powdered petals, and cheese. Reduce heat and keep stirring until cheese is completely melted.

Serve hot, over toast, or over rice or noodles.

FLOWER-BUD SAUCE

2 Tbs. butter	1 tsp. lemon juice
2 Tbs. flour	1 Tbs. chopped parsley
1 cup meat stock	⅓ cup pickled flower
¼ tsp. salt	buds, drained

Melt butter in small saucepan over low heat. Gradually stir in flour, and keep stirring until completely blended. Then gradually add stock, still stirring constantly. Stir in salt, lemon juice, and parsley. Keep stirring until sauce comes to a boil. Add pickled buds, and remove from heat.

Serve hot over meat or poultry.

Flower Jams, Jellies, and Preserves

§ Early English housewives lovingly outfitted their kitchen cupboards with all manner of flower jams, flower preserves, and flower jellies. The conserves adorned thin wafers for treats at teatime. But they were perhaps most treasured as additions to cakes, cookies, and elaborate old-fashioned English desserts.

It is interesting to contrast Mary Kettilby's method of preserving orange flowers with our modern adaptation. Here is the original version as it appeared in *A Collection of Above 300 Receipts in Cookery, Physick and Surgery* (1714):

Pick the flowers, and little oranges and ſtalks apart, boil the flowers in clear water till they are tender; boil the little oranges and ſtalks also in ſeveral waters, till the bitterneſs be quite gone: to a pound of flowers take 3 pounds of double-refined ʄugar, wet the ʄugar with water, and boil it to a ʄyrup; then drain the Flowers from their water, and put them into the ʄyrup, boil them a little, and put them into glaʄʄes.

The art of making flower jellies and jams has been cultivated for centuries by dedicated cooks of other countries. Rose-hip jam is a Swedish favorite and geranium-quince preserves are a Greek specialty. The Greeks also have an enticing recipe for rose-petal jelly, which is adapted in this chapter.

ROSE-HIP JAM
(Rose hips are the fruit of the rose)

1 qt. rose hips, well washed, with calyxes removed	1 qt. water 2 Tbs. lemon juice ⅔ lb. sugar

Place rose hips, water, and lemon juice in a large pan. Bring to a boil and continue boiling until hips are tender.

Crush the hips with a wooden spoon against the sides of the pan. To strain out the seeds, put hips through a food mill.

Place pulp in a saucepan and add sugar. Boil until candy thermometer reaches 220° F. Pour jam into sterilized screw-cap jars.

ROSE-PETAL JELLY

1 lb. rose petals	¾ cup water
1¾ lbs. sugar	1½ Tbs. lemon juice

Select petals from very fragrant roses. Take off the white tips. Wash petals and dry on paper towels.

Arrange petals and sugar in layers in a saucepan, starting with sugar on the bottom. Pour water over the petals and sugar; add lemon juice.

Slowly bring mixture to a boil. Simmer, covered, for 10 minutes. Test for doneness by dropping a little of the mixture onto a chilled dish. It should form a firm ball.

Take from heat and allow to cool, then pour into sterilized jars. Seal.

ROSE-GERANIUM JELLY

4½ lbs firm tart apples   Sugar
Water   8 rose-geranium leaves

Slice apples, but do not peel or core. Put apples in sturdy enamel saucepan with enough water to cover.

Bring to a boil and cook quickly until apples are soft. This will take about 20 minutes.

Allow apple juice to drip through a jelly bag without being forced.

Measure juice and place in a heavy saucepan with the rose-geranium leaves. Bring juice to a vigorous boil, then slowly add 1 cup sugar for each cup juice. Stir well. Boil until candy thermometer reaches 220°F. Remove geranium leaves.

Pour jelly into heated sterilized jars and seal immediately.

ORANGE-BLOSSOM PRESERVES

1 lb. orange blossoms   3 lbs. sugar
Water   3 cups water

Boil the flowers in water to cover until they are tender. Drain well and set aside.

In a large saucepan, moisten the sugar with 3 cups of water. Bring to a boil and cook 5 minutes to form a syrup.

Add the drained orange blossoms to syrup and cook 10 minutes.

Pack in heated sterilized jars and seal.

VIOLET JAM

1 cup violet petals	2⅔ cups sugar
1⅔ cups water	1 pkg. pectin

Separate stems and violet blossoms. Discard stems; then measure out 1 cup of blossoms.

Put blossoms and ⅔ cup water in electric blender. Mix on medium speed until paste is smooth.

Gradually add sugar. Continue blending until sugar is dissolved.

Add the pectin to 1 cup water in a saucepan. Boil 2 minutes, then add immediately to mixture in blender and blend well.

Pour violet jam into jars and seal. Refrigerate or freeze.

LIME-GERANIUM-QUINCE PRESERVES

1½ lbs. quince, peeled   1¼ cups water
    and coarsely grated   3 lime-geranium leaves
3 cups sugar   1 Tbs. lemon juice

Simmer quince in a large saucepan with sugar, water, and lime-geranium leaves for approximately 1 hour and 15 minutes. Stir frequently. Mixture should be the consistency of honey.

Add lemon juice during the last few minutes of cooking.

Remove geranium leaves. Pack in heated sterilized jars and seal.

LAVENDER-MINT JELLY

12 small jelly jars   ½ cup water
2 cups chopped mint   2½ cups apple juice
    leaves   Lavender blossoms
½ cup sugar   (approximately 12)
Green food coloring

Place chopped mint leaves in a small glass or enamel bowl. Add sugar which has been dissolved in water. Cover bowl tightly and let stand overnight.

Next morning, transfer mixture to a heavy saucepan and cook over medium heat until boiling point is reached, then strain. Mint juice is now ready to be used.

Heat apple juice until it reaches 220° F. (prepare as for Rose-Geranium Jelly (p. 158), omitting the geranium leaves). Add the mint juice and a few drops of green coloring.

Place a lavender blossom in the bottom of each heated sterilized jar.

Pour mint-apple mixture into jars and seal immediately. This yields approximately 12 small jelly jars.

ROSE JAM

1 lb. rose petals	1 pt. water
2½ lbs. sugar	1 Tbs. lemon juice

Use only petals of fragrant roses. Wash well.

Knead petals and 1 lb. of the sugar. Set aside and allow to stand overnight.

Put sugared petals in a kettle along with water and the remaining sugar. Cook quickly. Your candy thermometer should reach 225° F.

After jam is cooked, add the lemon juice and stir. Pour into sterilized jars and seal.

Sources of Illustrations

Publisher's Note: Most of the illustrations have been taken from ancient books and there is some uncertainty of varieties because of changes of nomenclature in modern times. Therefore, where names are available for varieties, the Latin name immediately following the common name is the older name, while the Latin name in parentheses is the modern equivalent, so far as can be determined. The initial letter in parentheses gives the key to the source of the illustration, as in the *Key to Sources* below.

24. Clove gilliflower (Carnation), *Dianthus caryophyllus*, (F.)

35. Briar rose, *Rosa canina*, (L.)

36. Lavender, *Lavandula spica*, (M.)

41. Common Borage, *Borago officinalis*, (M.)

45. Dandelion, *Leontodon taraxacum* (*Taraxacum officinale*) (F.)

46. Marigold (Calendula), *Calendula officinalis*, (J.)

52. *Day lily, Hemerocallis fulva*, (G.)

59. Marigold (Calendula) *Calendula officinalis*, (G.)

60. Endive chicory, *Cichorium intybus* (M.)

67. Carnation, *Dianthus caryophyllus*, (J.)

70. Cowslip, *Primula veris*, (Z.)

77. Tulip flowers, *Tulipa*

80. Orange, *Citrus aurantium**

100. Heliotrope *Heliotropium europaeum* (M.)

118. Sunflower *Helianthus annuus*, (G.)

121. Decorative illustration.[+]

130. Sweet violet, *viola odorata*, (M.)

135. Grape vine, *Vitis vinifera*

141. Wild Rose, (Z.)

142. Yellow violet (*Viola pedunculata?*), (G.)

148. Lemon, *Citrus limonia*, (G.)

153. Parsley, *Carum petroselinum* (Petroselinum hortense), (G.)

154. Rose*[+]
162. Purple iris, *Iris germanica*, (L.)

Key to Sources

(G.) John Gerarde, *The Herball*. London. 1597.

(J.) Thomas Johnson, Gerarde's *The Herball*, enlarged. London. 1633.

(M.) Petrus Andreus Matthiolus, *Commentari in libros sex Pedacii Dioscoridis*. Venice. 1554.

(L.) Matthias de L'Obel (or Lobel, or Lobelius), *Plantarum seu Stirpium Icones*. Antwerp, 1581.

(T.) R. J. Thornton, *A New Family Herbal*. London. 1810.

(Z.) Theodorus Zwinger, *Theatrum Botanicum*. Basle. 1744.

   * Source of illustration unknown.

   [+] Variety not certain or not given.

(L.M.) Jacques le Moyne, *La Clef des Champs*. 1586.

Index